Homemade Gooey Butter Cake Recipes

Over 50 variations of Gooey Butter Cake, made from scratch plus some cake mix versions.

Eleceia Cupps

Copyright

Preface

This cookbook has homemade recipes for Gooey Butter Cake as well as some that start off with a boxed cake mix. Gooey Butter Cake is a very rich and creamy dessert that starts with a cake-like crust then topped with a rich sweet cream cheese filling and baked until the top is golden. It's then cut into small squares like a bar cookie. The edges are chewy-crunchy and the center is soft and creamy. It's always been my favorite dessert and I wanted to see how many variations I could create.

Where the flavors came from: I started experimenting with various flavors and ingredients, adding fruit and nuts, spices, champagne, liqueurs, etc. I did a lot of research and came up with a list of complementing flavors that go well together like strawberry and banana, peaches and cinnamon, chocolate and peanut butter, etc. So using the trial and error method I came up with these recipes. I had to bake some of them more than once to get it right and one of them, Carrot Gooey Butter Cake took six tries but I finally got it the way I liked it. I also used some of my other favorite desserts and used those flavors as a base for a gooey butter cake too, like my Gingerbread with Lemon Cream Gooey Butter Cake and Pumpkin Pie Gooey Butter Cake. I even used my favorite cocktail from the Virgin Islands as the basis for my Caribbean Cocktail Gooey Butter Cake!

The book is divided into two sections:

Section 1: Recipes made-from-scratch start to finish

Section 2: Recipes start with a boxed cake mix and finished off from scratch.

Recipes Tips:

Ingredients
Using quality ingredients for the basics results in an excellent dessert. I like using real butter, large eggs and pure extracts instead of imitation.

Most of these recipes call for every day ingredients, nothing too exotic. The only ingredient you may not have in your pantry is espresso powder. If you already have it, great! If not and you bake a lot of chocolate goods you'll be pleased to see how much richer the chocolate flavor is when using espresso powder. Just a teaspoon or less is usually all you need. If you can't find it in your local baking supplies store you can always find it online, I got mine from Amazon. Be sure you buy *espresso powder for baking* rather than instant espresso coffee. The instant coffee will make it taste bitter since it's not designed for baking.

Measuring
When measuring out the dry ingredients, spoon lightly into the measuring cup then level off with a straight edge or small spatula rather than scooping out the flour with the measuring up. This can result in the flour packing down and adding more than the recipe calls for and making it dry.

Cooking Times and Oven Temperatures
Since all ovens bake a little different be sure and check it at the minimum time to be sure it doesn't overbake. Cooking times may vary depending on your oven, it could take longer to bake than times specified. The top should be a light gold color and have a slight jiggle in the center and the edges should bet set. Don't let it turn too brown or it will not be "gooey". The toothpick test doesn't work on Gooey Butter Cakes. Also if you're oven bakes unevenly rotate the pan halfway through cooking time for more even baking.

Recipe Variations

All the recipes are basically divided into two parts, the crust and the filling. I've paired up the crusts with the fillings that I thought complemented each other best. However you can swap crusts and fillings around to create some of your own versions as well.

The Butter
I used only real butter. If you substitute margarine for the butter it won't have the same flavor and richness this dessert is known for. Where it calls for melted butter, I cut up cold butter into 1" pieces and place them in a heat proof dish and microwave in 25 second intervals until it's almost melted and stir to help melt the rest. The key is not getting it too hot because you'll be adding egg to the mix and if the butter is too hot it can scramble the egg.

The Cream Cheese
To soften the cream cheese, place in the microwave about 30 seconds. It needs to be really soft, poke your finger in the middle and if it still has a chill, heat some more. If it's too cold when you beat it you'll end up with little solid pieces of cream cheese throughout your batter and you want the batter to be smooth. Be sure and scrape down the insides of the bowl to get it all mixed in.

The Extracts
Use pure extracts and flavorings. Several brands I like to use are Adams, McCormick, Watkins, Wilton and Totonac's (Mexican Vanilla). I'm not endorsing any particular brand so where you see a brand name listed it's because that's exactly what I used when I tested it in my kitchen and I was happy with the results. You can use any brand you like.

Freezing
These recipes freeze well so you can make ahead of time and let thaw to room temperature where the flavor is at its best and the texture is creamier.

Serving

What I like about all these desserts is they can be served straight from the pan they're baked in and most can be cut into bite size pieces and displayed on a pretty serving platter or tiered candy stand for special occasions. Gooey Butter Cake is one of those desserts that gets better with time. It's much better the next day so I'd recommend baking it the day before you plan to serve it or at least wait 4-6 hours so all those flavors can blend together to form that sweet gooey-ness. Store in the refrigerator but let it come to room temperature for serving. Most will be firm enough to cut into bars and eaten as finger food and a few are more like a pie so go ahead and use a fork.

These recipes are delicious and I hope you enjoy trying them and serving to your family and friends.

Table of Contents

Contents

Section 1 – Made from scratch

All recipes in this section are made-from-scratch start to finish.

A Basic Gooey Butter Cake Version 1

Basic gooey butter cake. A soft buttery crust with a creamy vanilla filling with just a hint of nutmeg. Simple and delicious!You will also find a cake mix version of this in Section 2 of the cookbook.

Ingredients

Bottom Layer:
2 cups all-purpose flour
1 cup granulated sugar
1 tablespoon baking powder
1 teaspoon salt
1 teaspoon vanilla extract
1 large egg, slightly beaten
10 tablespoons (1 stick plus 2 tablespoons) real butter, melted but not hot
2 tablespoons vegetable oil

Filling:
1 (8 ounce) package Creamcheese, softened

1/2 stick (4 tablespoons) real butter, very soft and slightly melted
2 large eggs
2 teaspoons vanilla extract
1/8 teaspoon freshly grated nutmeg, optional
3 cups powdered sugar

Directions
Preheat oven to 350F (177C). Grease the bottom and up the sides of a 9x13x2 baking pan.

Step 1: Make the bottom layer - A heavy duty or stand mixer is best for mixing the bottom layer as the mixture is thick.

Melt the butter in the microwave but don't let it get too hot. Melt partially then whisk or stir with a fork to melt the rest.

Into a large mixing bowl whisk together the flour, granulated sugar, baking powder and salt. With mixer on low speed add in melted butter and vegetable oil, beat until crumbly. Next beat in vanilla extract and the egg. Then turn up on high speed to mix completely until solid dough forms.

Transfer mixture into baking pan. Break up dough into pieces and distribute evenly in bottom of pan. Use knuckles to lightly "punch" dough around and into corners. With palm of hand press pieces down and together until it forms a solid and even bottom crust.

Step 2: Make the filling
Stir powdered sugar with a fork to aerate a little before measuring. Then spoon out into measuring cup, level off, place in medium bowl and set aside.

In a large bowl with electric mixer, beat softened Cream cheese and butter until smooth. On high speed beat in the 2 eggs one at a time and mix until mixture is creamy and smooth about 1 minute. Beat in the vanilla extract and nutmeg.

Lastly add the powdered sugar in small increments, beating slowly at first so sugar doesn't fly everywhere. Once all the sugar is moistened beat on high until smooth. Scrape down sides of bowl to get all the sugar mixed in.

Pour this mixture evenly over the bottom layer. Spread with the back of a spoon or spatula so batter touches the edges and corners of pan.

Place the pan in the oven and bake at 350 for about 29-30 minutes until golden on top. Don't over bake, it should be soft set in the center with a slight jiggle and the edges should be set. The center will firm up as it cools.

Allow to cool at least 1 hour at room temperature. Once it firms up, cut into small size pieces as they are very rich. Store tightly covered in the fridge or at room temperature. They taste best served at room temperature. Freezes well.

A BasicGooey Butter Cake Version 2

Basic gooey butter cake with a brown sugar crust. Topped with gooey vanilla filling with just a hint of nutmeg.

Ingredients

Bottom Layer:
2 cups all-purpose flour
1/2 cup granulated sugar
1/2 cup packed light brown sugar
1 tablespoon baking powder
1 teaspoon salt
1 teaspoon vanilla extract
2 large eggs, slightly beaten
1 stick real salted butter, melted but not hot
1/4 cup vegetable oil

Filling:
1 (8 ounce) package Creamcheese, softened
1/2 stick (4 tablespoons) real butter, very soft and slightly melted
2 large eggs

1/8 teaspoon freshly grated nutmeg
2 teaspoons vanilla extract
3 cups powdered sugar

Directions
Preheat oven to 350F (177C). Grease the bottom and up the sides of a 9x13x2 baking pan.

Step 1: Make the bottom layer - A heavy duty or stand mixer is best for mixing the bottom layer as the mixture is thick.

Melt the stick of butter in the microwave but don't let it get too hot. Melt partially then whisk or stir with a fork to melt the rest

Into a large mixing bowl whisk together the flour, granulated sugar, brown sugar, baking powder and salt. With mixer on low speed add in melted butter, vegetable oil, vanilla extract and the eggs. Then turn up on high speed to mix completely until a solid dough forms. Scrape down sides of bowl with spatula if needed.

Transfer mixture into baking pan. Break up dough into pieces and distribute evenly in bottom of pan. With palm of hand press pieces down and together until it forms a solid and even bottom crust.

Step 2: Make the filling
Stir powdered sugar with a fork to aerate a little before measuring. Then scoop out with measuring cup and level off. Place in medium bowl and set aside.

In a large bowl with electric mixer, beat softened Cream cheese and butter until smooth. Beat in the 2 eggs one at a time and mix until mixture is creamy and smooth. Beat in the nutmeg and vanilla extract. Mix about 1 minute until well combined.

Lastly add the powdered sugar in small increments, beating slowly at first so sugar doesn't fly everywhere. Once all the sugar is moistened beat on high until smooth. Scrape down sides of bowl to get all the sugar mixed in.

Pour this mixture evenly over the bottom layer. Spread with the back of a spoon or spatula so batter touches the edges and corners of pan.

Place the pan in the oven and bake at 350 for about 29-30 minutes until golden on top. Don't over bake, it should be soft set in the center with a slight jiggle and the edges should be set. The center will firm up as it cools.

Allow to cool at least 1 hour at room temperature. Once it firms up, cut into small size pieces as they are very rich. Store tightly covered in the fridge or at room temperature. They taste best served at room temperature. Freezes well.

A Chocolate Gooey Butter Cake

A rich chocolate crust made with sweet melted baking chocolate then filled with a creamy chocolate cocoa filling. You will also find a cake mix version of this in Section 2 of this cookbook.

Ingredients

Bottom layer
2 cups all-purpose flour
1 cup granulated sugar
1 tablespoon baking powder
1/2 teaspoon salt
1 stick real unsalted butter, melted but not hot
1 large egg, slightly beaten

18

1 (4-ounce) bar German's sweet baking chocolate, chopped
into 1/2-inch pieces
1 teaspoon vanilla extract

Filling:
1 (8 ounce) package Creamcheese, softened
1/2 stick (4 tablespoons) real butter, very soft and slightly
melted
2 large eggs
1 teaspoon vanilla extract
1/3 cup powdered baking cocoa
3-1/4 cups powdered sugar

Directions
Preheat oven to 350F (177C). Grease the bottom and up the
sides of a 9x13x2 baking pan.

Step 1: Make the bottom layer -A heavy duty or stand mixer
is best for mixing the bottom layer as the mixture is thick.

Melt the chocolate by placing the pieces in a very lightly
greased microwave safe glass bowl. Heat it on medium high
for about 1 minute to start with. Remove from the microwave
and stir. Repeat heating at shorter intervals, 15 to 20 seconds,
stirring in between, until the chocolate is completely melted
and has a smooth consistency. Do not overheat or get any
water in the chocolate. Remove the bowl from microwave and
set aside until ready to use.

Melt the stick of butter in the microwave but don't let it get too
hot. Melt partially then whisk or stir with a fork to melt the rest.

Into a large mixing bowl whisk together the flour, granulated
sugar, baking powder and salt. With mixer on low speed add
in melted butter and egg. Then turn up on high speed to mix
completely until crumbly. Scrape down sides of bowl with
spatula if needed. With mixer on low, beat in melted chocolate
and vanilla extract, mixing well.

19

Transfer dough to prepared baking pan. With a rubber spatula spread out the dough and lightly pat down until a solid bottom crust forms.

Step 2: Make the filling

Stir powdered sugar with a fork to aerate a little before measuring. Then spoon out into measuring cup, level off, place in medium bowl. Whisk in the 1/3 cup cocoa and set aside.

In a large bowl with electric mixer, beat softened Cream cheese and the 4 tablespoons. softened butter until smooth. Beat in the 2 eggs one at a time and mix until mixture is creamy and smooth. Beat in the vanilla extract.

Lastly add the powdered sugar/cocoa mixture in small increments, beating slowly at first so the powdered mixture doesn't fly everywhere. Once all the sugar/cocoa is moistened beat on high until smooth. Scrape down sides of bowl often to get all the sugar/cocoa mixed in.

Pour this mixture evenly over the bottom layer. Spread with the back of a spoon or spatula so batter touches the edges and corners of pan.

Place the pan in the oven and bake at 350 for about 29-30 minutes until a top looks dry, see pic below. It will look just like a chocolate cake on top and it should be soft set in the center with a slight jiggle. The center will firm up as it cools.

Allow to cool at least 1 hour at room temperature. Once it firms up, cut into small size pieces as they are very rich. Store tightly covered in the fridge or at room temperature. I think they taste best served at room temperature. Dust the top with a sprinkle of powdered sugar just before serving if desired. Freezes well.

Apple Spice Gooey Bars

A spiced soft bottom crust filled with a creamy apple flavored filling using apple juice concentrate. Then topped with a crispy crumb topping.

Ingredients

Bottom Layer:
2 cups all-purpose flour
1 cup granulated sugar
1 tablespoon baking powder
1 teaspoon ground cinnamon
1/2 teaspoon ground nutmeg
1/2 teaspoon ground cloves
1 teaspoon salt
1 teaspoon vanilla extract

1 large egg, slightly beaten
10 tablespoons (1 stick plus 2 tablespoons) real butter, melted
but not hot
2 tablespoons vegetable oil

Filling:
1 (8 ounce) package Creamcheese, softened
1/2 stick (4 tablespoons) real butter, very soft and slightly
melted
2 large eggs
1 tablespoon tapioca flour
1/2 cup thawed frozen apple juice concentrate, do not mix with
water use full strength
1 teaspoon vanilla extract
3 cups powdered sugar
Prepared Crumb topping, recipe follows (optional)

Directions
Preheat oven to 350F (177C). Grease the bottom and up the
sides of a 9x13x2 baking pan.

Step 1: Make the bottom layer - A heavy duty or stand
mixer is best for mixing the bottom layer as the mixture is
thick.

Melt the butter in the microwave but don't let it get too hot.
Melt partially then whisk or stir with a fork to melt the rest.

Into a large mixing bowl whisk together the flour, sugar, baking
powder, spices and salt. With mixer on low speed add in
melted butter and vegetable oil, beat until crumbly. Next beat
in vanilla extract and the egg. Then turn up on high speed to
mix completely until solid dough forms.

Transfer mixture to baking pan. Break up dough into pieces
and distribute evenly in bottom of pan. With palm of hand
press pieces down and together until it forms a solid and even
bottom crust.

Step 2: Make the crumb topping, optional
1/2 cup granulated sugar
1/4 cup flour
1/4 teaspoon ground cinnamon
2 tablespoons butter

In a medium bowl whisk together the sugar, flour and cinnamon.
With a pastry cutter or food processor cut the butter into flour mixture until consistency is like fine bread crumbs or sand. Or you can just rub mixture between your fingers and thumb to mix the butter into the dry mixture. Once it's crumbly rub mixture between your hands until it feels like sand. (See image below.) Store in fridge until ready to use.

Step 3: Make the filling
Stir powdered sugar with a fork to aerate a little before measuring. Then scoop out with measuring cup and level off. Place in medium bowl and set aside.

In a large bowl with electric mixer, beat softened Cream cheese and butter until smooth. Beat in the 2 eggs one at a time and mix until mixture is creamy and smooth. Beat in the tapioca flour, apple juice concentrate and vanilla extract.

Lastly add the powdered sugar in small increments, beating slowly at first so sugar doesn't fly everywhere. Once all the sugar is moistened beat on high until smooth. Scrape down sides of bowl to get all the sugar mixed in.

Pour this mixture evenly over the bottom layer. Spread with the back of a spoon or spatula so batter touches the edges and corners of pan.

If using the crumb topping, lightly sprinkle the crumb topping over the top and using the tins of a fork, gently spread it evenly over the batter.

Place the pan in the oven and bake at 350 for 30-32 minutes until a rich golden color on top. If you added the crumb topping it should be a nice golden brown and crispy. Don't over bake, it should be soft set in the center with a slight jiggle and the edges should be set. The center will firm up as it cools.

Allow to cool at least 1 hour at room temperature. Once it firms up, cut into small size pieces as they are very rich. Store tightly covered in the fridge or at room temperature. I think they taste best served at room temperature. Freezes well.

Banana & Peanut Butter Gooey Bars

Soft banana cake crust with a creamy peanut butter filling drizzled with chocolate fudge sauce.

Ingredients

Bottom Layer:
2 cups all-purpose flour
1 cup granulated sugar
1 tablespoon baking powder
1 teaspoon salt
1 teaspoon vanilla extract
1 large egg, slightly beaten
10 tablespoons (1 stick plus 2 tablespoons) real butter, melted but not hot
2 tablespoons vegetable oil
1/2 cup mashed bananas, about 2 medium overripe bananas

Filling:
1 (8 ounce) package Creamcheese, softened
1/2 stick (4 tablespoons) real butter, very soft and slightly melted
2/3 cup smooth peanut butter

2 large eggs
1 teaspoon vanilla extract
1/4 teaspoon McCormick's banana extract
3 cups powdered sugar
Prepared Chocolate Fudge Sauce, recipe follows or use store bought ice cream topping

Directions

Preheat oven to 350F (177C). Grease the bottom and up the sides of a 9x13x2 baking pan.

Note: If making the fudge sauce homemade, make it ahead of time as it needs time to cool and thicken. Recipe follows.

Step 1: Make the bottom layer -A heavy duty or stand mixer is best for mixing the bottom layer as the mixture is thick.

Melt the butter in the microwave but don't let it get too hot. Melt partially then whisk or stir with a fork to melt the rest.

Into a large mixing bowl whisk together the flour, sugar, baking powder and salt. With mixer on low speed add in melted butter and vegetable oil, beat until crumbly. Beat in mashed bananas until dough forms. Next beat in vanilla extract and the egg. Then turn up on high speed to mix completely.

Transfer mixture into baking pan. With a rubber spatula spread out evenly over the bottom of the pan.

Step 2: Make the filling
Stir powdered sugar with a fork to aerate a little before measuring. Then spoon out into measuring cup, level off, place in medium bowl and set aside.

In a large bowl with electric mixer, beat softened Cream cheese, butter and peanut butter until smooth. Beat in the 2 eggs one at a time mixing well after each addition. Beat until creamy and smooth. Beat in the vanilla and banana extract.

Lastly add the powdered sugar in small increments, beating slowly at first so sugar doesn't fly everywhere. Once all the sugar is moistened beat on high until smooth. You may need to scrape down sides of bowl to get all the sugar mixed in.

Pour this mixture evenly over the bottom layer. Spread with the back of a spoon or spatula so batter touches the edges and corners of pan.

Place the pan in the oven and bake at 350 for about 28-29 minutes until a golden color on top. Don't over bake, it should be soft set in the center and have a slight jiggle.
The center will firm up as it cools.

Allow to cool at least 1 hour at room temperature. Once it firms up, cut into small size pieces as they are very rich. Before serving drizzle with chocolate sauce if desired. Store tightly covered in the fridge or at room temperature. I think they taste best served at room temperature.

Homemade Chocolate Fudge Sauce (yields about 2/3 cups)

1/2 cup sugar
2 tablespoons cocoa powder
1/8 teaspoon salt
1/4 cup water
2 tablespoons butter
1 tablespoon evaporated or regular milk
1 teaspoon vanilla extract

Directions
Combine sugar, cocoa, and salt in small saucepan. Whisk in water. Bring to a boil over medium high heat. Add butter and stirring constantly let boil for 1 minute over medium heat. Remove from heat and whisk in milk until smooth. Stir in vanilla extract. Pour into a heat proof cup or bowl to cool down. I use a small Pyrex measuring cup. The mixture will be thin but will thicken as it cools. Once it reaches room temperature store covered in fridge until ready to use. Stir well

before drizzling. Keep refrigerated up to a week or freeze leftovers up to two months.

Banana Cream Gooey Bars

This has a soft banana cake crust topped with creamy, gooey banana filling.

Ingredients

Bottom Layer:
2 cups all-purpose flour
1 cup granulated sugar
1 tablespoon baking powder
1 teaspoon salt
1 teaspoon vanilla extract
1 large egg, slightly beaten
10 tablespoons (1 stick plus 2 tablespoons) real butter, melted but not hot
2 tablespoons vegetable oil
1/2 cup mashed bananas, about 2 medium very ripe bananas

Filling:
1 (8 ounce) package Cream cheese, very softened
1/2 stick (4 tablespoons) real butter, partially melted

2 large eggs
1/2 teaspoon McCormick's banana extract
1/4 teaspoon vanilla extract
3 cups powdered sugar
5 drops yellow food coloring, optional

Directions
Preheat oven to 350F (177C). Grease the bottom and up the sides of a 9x13x2 baking pan.

Step 1: Make the bottom layer - A heavy duty or stand mixer is best for mixing the bottom layer as the mixture is thick.

Melt the butter in the microwave but don't let it get too hot. Melt partially then whisk or stir with a fork to melt the rest.

Into a large mixing bowl whisk together the flour, sugar, baking powder and salt. With mixer on low speed add in melted butter and vegetable oil, beat until crumbly. Beat in mashed bananas until dough forms. Next beat in vanilla extract and the egg. Then turn up on high speed to mix completely.

Transfer mixture into baking pan. With a rubber spatula spread out evenly over the bottom of the pan.

Step 2: Make the filling
Stir powdered sugar to aerate a little before measuring then spoon out into measuring cup and level off with a flat edge; Place in medium size bowl and set aside.

In a large bowl with electric mixer, beat Cream cheese and butter until smooth. Add the two eggs one at a time and beat until creamy and smooth. Beat in the extracts.

Lastly add the powdered sugar in small increments, beating slowly at first then beat on high until smooth. You may need to scrape down sides of bowl to get all the sugar mixed in. If using food coloring, add now until mixture is a pale yellow.

Pour this mixture evenly over the bottom layer. Spread with the back of a spoon or spatula so batter touches the edges and corners of pan.

Place the pan in the oven and bake 28-30 minutes until a rich golden on top. Don't over bake, the edges should be set but the center should have a slight jiggle. The center will firm up as it cools.

Allow to cool at least 1 hour at room temperature. Once it firms up, cut into small size pieces as they are very rich. Bars can be stored at room temperature or kept in the fridge. Flavor is best when served at room temperature.

Bananas Foster Gooey Butter Cake

Get all the flavor of the decadent bananas foster dessert - without the flame - in each gooey bite! A pleasing texture as you bite through a crispy cinnamony topping then a creamy banana filling over a soft nutty banana cake crust.

Ingredients

Bottom Layer:
2 cups all-purpose flour
1 cup granulated sugar
1 tablespoon baking powder
1/8 teaspoon cinnamon
1 teaspoon salt
1 teaspoon vanilla extract
1 large egg, slightly beaten
10 tablespoons (1 stick plus 2 tablespoons) real butter, melted but not hot
2 tablespoons vegetable oil
1/2 cup mashed bananas, about 2 medium very ripe bananas
1/3 cup chopped walnuts or pecans

Filling:
1 (8 ounce) package cream cheese, very softened
1/2 stick (4 tablespoons) real butter, partially melted
2 large eggs
1/8 teaspoon cinnamon
Dash of nutmeg
1/2 teaspoon McCormick's banana extract
1/2 teaspoon rum extract
1/2 teaspoon vanilla extract
3 cups powdered sugar
3 drops yellow food coloring, optional
Caramel ice cream topping, optional

Directions
Preheat oven to 350F (177C). Grease the bottom and up the sides of a 9x13x2 baking pan.

Step 1: Make the bottom layer - A heavy duty or stand mixer is best for mixing the bottom layer as the mixture is thick.

Melt the butter in the microwave until partially melted. Whisk or stir with a fork to melt the rest until completely liquid. Set aside.

In a large mixing bowl whisk together flour, sugar, baking powder, cinnamon and salt. Beat in melted butter, vegetable oil and mashed bananas. With mixer on low speed mix just until everything is combined, scraping bowl occasionally. Beat in the egg and vanilla extract. Lastly beat in the nuts until well incorporated, scrape down sides of bowl with spatula if needed. Then turn up on high speed to mix completely.

Transfer dough mixture to baking pan and using a rubber spatula, spread out evenly in bottom of pan.

Step 2: Make the crumb topping

1/2 cup granulated sugar or lightly packed brown sugar
1/4 cup flour
1/4 teaspoon ground cinnamon
1/8 teaspoon ground nutmeg
2 tablespoons butter

In a medium bowl whisk together the sugar, flour and spices. With a pastry cutter or food processor cut the butter into flour mixture until consistency is like fine bread crumbs or sand. Or you can just rub mixture between your fingers and thumb to mash the butter into the dry mixture. Once it's crumbly, rub mixture back and forth between both your palms until it resembles sand. Store in fridge until ready to use. See image below.

Step 3: Make the filling
Stir powdered sugar to aerate a little before measuring then spoon out into measuring cup and level off with a flat edge; Place in medium size bowl and set aside.

In a large bowl with electric mixer, beat cream cheese and butter until smooth. Add the two eggs one at a time and beat until creamy and smooth. Beat in cinnamon, nutmeg and all the extracts until well blended.

Lastly add the powdered sugar in small increments, beating slowly at first then beat on high until smooth. You may need to scrape down sides of bowl to get all the sugar mixed in. If using food coloring add it now until batter is a very pale yellow.

Pour this mixture evenly over the bottom layer. Spread with the back of a spoon or spatula so batter touches the edges and corners of pan.

Sprinkle crumb topping evenly over the cream cheese mixture. Very lightly with tins of a fork spread crumbs evenly over top and to the corners and edges. Do not shake pan side to side to try to even out crumbs, the raw batter will slosh over the crumbs.

Place the pan in the oven and bake about 30-35 minutes. When done the center will be soft set and jiggle slightly and the crumb topping should be lightly browned and crisp. The edges will be a light brown and set, edges shouldn't jiggle. The center will firm up as it cools

Allow to cool at least 1 hour at room temperature. Once it firms up, cut into small size pieces as they are very rich. If desired, cover the bars with a very thin drizzle of caramel sauce (if using), use sparingly as they are already very rich. I like them just plain because they are already very flavorful but the drizzle looks really nice for serving. Store in the refrigerator but serve at room temperature.

Blueberry Almond Gooey Bars

*Bottom crust with almonds then filled with a creamy topping
full of fresh blueberries*

Ingredients

Bottom Layer:
2 cups all-purpose flour
1/2 cup granulated sugar
1/2 cup packed light brown sugar
1 tablespoon baking powder
1/2 teaspoon salt
1/3 cup finely chopped blanched slivered almonds
1 stick real unsalted butter, melted but not hot
1/4 cup vegetable oil
1 teaspoon vanilla extract
2 large eggs

Filling:
1 (8 ounce) package Creamcheese, softened

1/2 stick (4 tablespoons) real butter, very soft and slightly melted
2 large eggs
1 teaspoon vanilla extract
1/2 teaspoon almond extract
3 cups powdered sugar
1 pint (about 1-1/2 cups) fresh blueberries, rinsed and dry

Directions
Preheat oven to 350F (177C). Grease the bottom and up the sides of a 9x13x2 baking pan. Be sure to grease the pan all the way up the sides as the blueberries will glue themselves to any dry spots on the pan.

Step 1: Make the bottom layer -A heavy duty or stand mixer is best for mixing the bottom layer as the mixture is thick.

Chop the almonds by pulsing a few times in a food processor or crush in a plastic bag.

Melt the stick of butter in the microwave but don't let it get too hot. Melt partially then whisk or stir with a fork to melt the rest.

Into a large mixing bowl whisk together the flour, granulated sugar, brown sugar, baking powder and salt. With mixer on low speed add in melted butter, vegetable oil, vanilla extract and the eggs. Then turn up on high speed and mix completely until a solid dough forms. Scrape down sides of bowl with spatula if needed. Beat in the chopped almonds.

Transfer mixture to baking pan. Break up dough into pieces and distribute evenly in bottom of pan. With palm of hand press pieces down and together until it forms a solid and even bottom crust.

Step 2: Make the filling

Stir powdered sugar with a fork to aerate a little before measuring. Then scoop out with measuring cup and level off. Place in medium bowl and set aside.

In a large bowl with electric mixer, beat softened Cream cheese and butter until smooth. Beat in the 2 eggs one at a time and mix until mixture is creamy and smooth. Beat in the extracts.

Lastly add the powdered sugar in small increments, beating slowly at first so sugar doesn't fly everywhere. Once all the sugar is moistened beat on high until smooth. Scrape down sides of bowl to get all the sugar mixed in. By hand, gently stir in the blueberries.

Pour this mixture evenly over the bottom layer. Spread with the back of a spoon or spatula so batter touches the edges and corners of pan.

Place the pan in the oven and bake at 350 for about 30-35 minutes or until golden on top. Don't over bake, it should be soft set in the center with a slight jiggle. The center will firm up as it cools.

Allow to cool at least 1 hour at room temperature. Once it firms up, cut into small size pieces as they are very rich. Store tightly covered in the fridge. I think they taste best served at room temperature. Freezes well.

Butterscotch Gooey Bars

Delicious nutty butterscotch crust topped with a sweet cream cheese filling

Ingredients

Bottom Layer:
12 tablespoons (1-1/2 stick) butter
1 cup packed brown sugar
2 cups all-purpose flour
2 teaspoons baking powder
1/2 teaspoon kosher salt
1 teaspoon vanilla extract
1 tablespoon vegetable oil
1/3 cup chopped pecans
1 large egg, slightly beaten

Filling:
1 (8 ounce) package Cream Cheese, softened
1/2 stick (4 tablespoons) real butter, very soft and slightly melted
2 large eggs
2 teaspoons vanilla extract
3 cups powdered sugar

Directions
Preheat oven to 350F (177C). Grease the bottom and up the sides of a 9x13x2 baking pan.

Step 1: Make the bottom layer - works best with a stand mixer as the mix is thick.
Melt the butter in a medium saucepan until bubbly. Stir in the brown sugar, return to boil and cook on medium heat and cook and stir for 2 minutes. Remove from heat and transfer mixture to large mixing bowl.

Sift together the flour, baking powder and salt. Add this to the sugar/butter mixture and mix until well blended.

Next beat in vanilla extract, vegetable oil and pecans. Test mixture and be sure it's no longer hot before adding in the egg. Beat in egg until mixture is moist and crumbly.
Transfer to baking pan. Spread out dough evenly with hands then press down until dough forms a solid and even bottom crust. Set aside.

Step 2: Make the filling
Stir powdered sugar with a fork to aerate a little before measuring. Then scoop out with measuring cup and level off. Place in medium bowl and set aside.

In a large bowl with electric mixer, beat softened cream cheese and butter until smooth. Beat in the 2 eggs one at a time and mix until mixture is creamy and smooth. Scrape down sides of bowl to get all the cream cheese mixed in. Beat in the vanilla extract. Mix about 1 minute until well combined.

Lastly add the powdered sugar in small increments, beating slowly at first so sugar doesn't fly everywhere. Once all the sugar is moistened beat on high until smooth. Scrape down sides of bowl to get all the sugar mixed in.

Pour this mixture evenly over the bottom layer. Spread with the back of a spoon or spatula so batter touches the edges and corners of pan.

Place the pan in the oven and bake at 350 for about 30-35 minutes until golden on top. Don't over bake, the edges should be set and it should be soft set in the center with a slight jiggle. The center will firm up as it cools.

Allow to cool at least 1 hour at room temperature. Once it firms up, cut into small size pieces as they are very rich. Store tightly covered in the fridge or at room temperature. They taste best served at room temperature. Freezes well.

Caramel Cappuccino Gooey Bites

Soft bottom crust with a filling made with homemade caramel sauce and espresso for that perfect Cappuccino flavor in every luscious gooey bite!

Ingredients

Bottom Layer:
2 cups all-purpose flour
1/2 cup granulated sugar
1/2 cup packed light brown sugar
1 tablespoon baking powder
1 teaspoon cinnamon
1 teaspoon salt
1 teaspoon vanilla extract
2 large eggs, slightly beaten
1 stick real salted butter, melted but not hot
1/4 cup vegetable oil

Filling:
1 (8 ounce) package Creamcheese, softened
1/2 stick (4 tablespoons) real butter, very soft and slightly melted
1/2 cup caramel ice cream topping or make from scratch, * recipe follows
2 large eggs

*1-1/8 teaspoon espresso powder (or up to 1-1/2 teaspoon for a stronger coffee flavor)
1-1/2 teaspoons vanilla extract
3 cups powdered sugar

Directions

* Be sure to use espresso powder <u>for baking</u> versus instant espresso coffee granules. Using coffee granules will make it taste bitter.

If making caramel topping from scratch, do ahead of time as it needs time to cool and thicken, recipe follows.

Preheat oven to 350F (177C). Grease the bottom and up the sides of a 9x13x2 baking pan.

Step 1: Make the bottom layer - A heavy duty or stand mixer is best for mixing the bottom layer as the mixture is thick.

Melt the stick of butter in the microwave but don't let it get too hot. Melt partially then whisk or stir with a fork to melt the rest.

Into a large mixing bowl whisk together the flour, granulated sugar, brown sugar, baking powder, cinnamon and salt. With mixer on low speed add in melted butter, vegetable oil, vanilla extract and the eggs. Then turn up on high speed to mix completely until a solid dough forms. Scrape down sides of bowl with spatula if needed.

Transfer mixture into baking pan. Break up dough into pieces and distribute evenly in bottom of pan. With palm of hand press pieces down and together until it forms a solid and even bottom crust.

Step 2: Make the filling

Stir powdered sugar with a fork to aerate a little before measuring. Then scoop out with measuring cup and level off. Place in medium bowl and set aside.

In a large bowl with electric mixer, beat softened Cream cheese, butter and caramel topping until smooth. Beat in the 2 eggs one at a time and mix until mixture is creamy and smooth. Beat in the espresso powder and vanilla extract. Mix about 1 minute until well combined.

Lastly add the powdered sugar in small increments, beating slowly at first so sugar doesn't fly everywhere. Once all the sugar is moistened beat on high until smooth. Scrape down sides of bowl to get all the sugar mixed in.

Pour this mixture evenly over the bottom layer. Spread with the back of a spoon or spatula so batter touches the edges and corners of pan.

Place the pan in the oven and bake at 350 for about 28-29 minutes until golden on top. Don't over bake, it should be soft set in the center with a slight jiggle and the edges should be set. The center will firm up as it cools.

Allow to cool at least 1 hour at room temperature. Once it firms up, cut into small size pieces as they are very rich. Store tightly covered in the fridge or at room temperature. I think they taste best served at room temperature. Freezes well.

If desired, just before serving you can dust the top with powdered sugar then drizzle a very thin stream of warm caramel over the top.

Homemade Caramel sauce:

1/4 cup real butter, don't sub margarine
Dash salt
1/2 cup packed brown sugar
1/3 cup heavy whipping cream

1 teaspoon vanilla extract

Directions
1. In a small saucepan melt butter and salt.
2. Add the brown sugar; whisk and cook on medium heat until combined and thickened, about a minute or so.
3. Whisk in the whipping cream until thoroughly blended and heated about another minute.
4. Remove from heat
5. Whisk in vanilla until well combined.
6. Let come to room temperature. Stir with a fork if it starts to separate as it thickens. Then store in fridge until chilled and thick. Stir before using.

This makes almost a cup of sauce, a little more than you'll need for this recipe.

Caramel Spice Gooey Bars

Warm spiced crust with a creamy homemade caramel filling.

Ingredients

Bottom Layer:
2 cups all-purpose flour
1/2 cup granulated sugar
1/2 cup packed light brown sugar
1 tablespoon baking powder
1 teaspoon ground cinnamon
1/2 teaspoon ground nutmeg
1/2 teaspoon ground cloves
1/2 teaspoon salt
1 teaspoon vanilla extract

2 large eggs, slightly beaten
1 stick real unsalted butter, melted but not hot
1/4 cup vegetable oil

Filling:
1 (8 ounce) package Creamcheese, softened
1/2 stick (4 tablespoons) real butter, very soft and slightly melted
1/2 cup caramel sauce ice cream topping or you can make from scratch, *recipe follows
Dash of salt
2 large eggs
1 teaspoon vanilla extract
3 cups powdered sugar

Directions
* If making caramel topping from scratch, do ahead of time as it needs time to cool and thicken, recipe follows.

Preheat oven to 350F (177C). Grease the bottom and up the sides of a 9x13x2 baking pan.

Step 1: Make the bottom layer - A heavy duty or stand mixer is best for mixing the bottom layer as the mixture is thick.

Melt butter in the microwave but don't let it get too hot. Melt partially then whisk or stir with a fork to melt the rest.

Into a large mixing bowl whisk together the flour, granulated sugar, brown sugar, baking powder, cinnamon, nutmeg, cloves and salt. With mixer on low speed add in melted butter, vegetable oil, vanilla extract and the eggs. Then turn up on high speed to mix completely until a solid dough forms. Scrape down sides of bowl with spatula if needed.

Transfer mixture into baking pan. Break up dough into pieces and distribute evenly in bottom of pan. With palm of hand

press pieces down and together until it forms a solid and even bottom crust.

Step 2: Make the filling

Stir powdered sugar with a fork to aerate a little before measuring. Then scoop out with measuring cup and level off. Place in medium bowl and set aside.

In a large bowl with electric mixer, beat softened Cream cheese and butter until smooth. Then add caramel sauce and beat until smooth. Beat in the dash of salt and 2 eggs one at a time and mix until mixture is creamy and smooth. Scrape down sides of bowl with spatula to get all mixed in well. Beat in the vanilla extract.

Lastly add the powdered sugar in small increments, beating slowly at first so sugar doesn't fly everywhere. Once all the sugar is moistened beat on high until smooth. Scrape down sides of bowl to get all the sugar mixed in.

Pour this mixture evenly over the bottom layer. Spread with the back of a spoon or spatula so batter touches the edges and corners of pan.

Place the pan in the oven and bake at 350 for about 28-30 minutes until golden color on top. Don't over bake, it should be soft set in the center with a slight jiggle and the edges should be set. The center will firm up as it cools.

Allow to cool at least 1 hour at room temperature. Once firm, cut into small size pieces as they are very rich. Store tightly covered in the fridge or at room temperature. I think they taste best served at room temperature. Freezes well.

Homemade Caramel sauce:

1/4 cup real butter, don't sub margarine
Dash salt
1/2 cup packed brown sugar

1/3 cup heavy whipping cream
1 teaspoon vanilla extract

Directions
1. In a small saucepan melt butter and salt.
2. Add the brown sugar; whisk and cook on medium heat until combined and thickened, about a minute or so.
3. Whisk in the whipping cream until thoroughly blended and heated about another minute.
4. Remove from heat
5. Whisk in vanilla until well combined.
6. Let come to room temperature. Stir with a fork if it starts to separate as it thickens. Then store in fridge until chilled and thick. Stir before using.

This makes almost a cup of sauce, a little more than you'll need for this recipe.

Carrot Gooey Butter Cake Bars

A warm spiced crust topped with a filling made with fresh carrots and orange juice. This tastes like a sweet carrot casserole with the crust baked in!

Ingredients

<u>Bottom Layer:</u>
2 cups all-purpose flour
1 cup granulated sugar
1 tablespoon baking powder
1 teaspoon salt
1/2 teaspoon cinnamon
1/4 teaspoon nutmeg
1/8 teaspoon cloves
1 teaspoon vanilla extract
1 large egg, slightly beaten
10 tablespoons (1 stick plus 2 tablespoons) real butter, melted but not hot
2 tablespoons vegetable oil
2 tablespoons pureed carrots

Filling:
1 (8 ounce) package Creamcheese, softened
1/2 stick (4 tablespoons) real butter, very soft and slightly melted
2 large eggs
2/3 cups cooked and pureed carrots
2 tablespoons fresh squeezed orange juice
2 teaspoons tapioca flour
1/8 teaspoon of ground ginger
1 teaspoon vanilla extract
3 cups powdered sugar

Directions
Preheat oven to 325F. Grease the bottom and up the sides of a 9x13x2 baking pan.

Step 1: Cook carrots
Peel and thinly slice 5 or 6 large carrots and boil until tender. Drain and puree' in blender or food processor until smooth. Measure out 2/3 cups and 2 tablespoons, divided and set aside.

Step 2: Make the bottom layer - A heavy duty or stand mixer is best for mixing the bottom layer as the mixture is thick.

Melt the butter in the microwave but don't let it get too hot. Melt partially then whisk or stir with a fork to melt the rest.

Into a large mixing bowl whisk together the flour, granulated sugar, baking powder, salt and the spices. With mixer on low speed add in melted butter and vegetable oil, beat until crumbly. Next beat in the 2 tablespoons of carrots, vanilla extract and the egg. Then turn up on high speed to mix completely until solid dough forms.

Transfer mixture into baking pan. Break up dough into pieces and distribute evenly in bottom of pan. With palm of hand

press pieces down and together until it forms a solid and even bottom crust.

Step 3: Make the filling
Stir powdered sugar with a fork to aerate a little before measuring. Then scoop out with measuring cup and level off. Place in medium bowl and set aside.

In a large bowl with electric mixer, beat softened cream cheese and butter until smooth. Beat in the 2 eggs one at a time and mix until creamy and smooth. Beat in the pureed carrots, orange juice, vanilla extract, tapioca flour and ginger until smooth and creamy.

Lastly add the powdered sugar in small increments, beating slowly at first so sugar doesn't fly everywhere. Once all the sugar is moistened beat on high until smooth. Scrape down sides of bowl to get all the sugar mixed in.

Pour this mixture evenly over the bottom layer. Spread with the back of a spoon or spatula so batter touches the edges and corners of pan.

Place the pan in the oven and bake at 325F for about 35-40 minutes until light golden on top. Don't over bake, the edges should be set and soft set in the center with a slight jiggle. The center will firm up as it cools. Allow to cool at least 1 hour at room temperature. Store tightly covered in the fridge. Delicious for the holidays. If desired, just before serving sprinkle with a little powdered sugar. Freezes well.

Cherry Cream Gooey Butter Cake

A pleasing texture as you bite into a crispy topping then a creamy filling full of cherries over a soft crust. Recipe also includes a 'blueberry' alternative.

Ingredients

Bottom Layer:
2 cups all-purpose flour
1 cup granulated sugar
1 tablespoon baking powder
1 teaspoon salt
1 teaspoon vanilla extract
1 large egg, slightly beaten
10 tablespoons (1 stick plus 2 tablespoons) real butter, melted but not hot
2 tablespoons vegetable oil

Filling:

5 oz. package (1 cup) dried cherries, plumped and drained (directions follow)
1 (8 ounce) package Creamcheese, softened
4 tablespoons real butter, very soft and slightly melted
Dash of salt
2 large eggs
1 teaspoon vanilla extract
1/2 teaspoon almond extract, I used Adams
2-1/2 cups powdered sugar
Prepared Crumb topping, recipe follows

Directions
Preheat oven to 350F (177C). Grease the bottom and up the sides of a 9x13x2 baking pan.

Step 1: Make the crumb topping and store in refrigerator until ready to use:

1/2 cup granulated sugar
1/4 cup flour
1/4 teaspoon ground cinnamon
1/8 teaspoon ground nutmeg
2 tablespoons butter

In a medium bowl whisk together the sugar, flour and spices. With a pastry cutter or food processor cut the butter into flour mixture until consistency is like fine bread crumbs or sand. Or you can just rub mixture between your fingers and thumb to mash the butter into the dry mixture. Once it's crumbly rub mixture between your hands until it resembles sand. Store in fridge until ready to use. See image below.

Step 2: Plump the cherries:
In a small pot cover the dried cherries with water and boil for 2 minutes until they plump. Remove from water and drain well. Set aside.

Step 3: Make the bottom layer - A heavy duty or stand mixer is best for mixing the bottom layer as the mixture is thick.

Melt the butter in the microwave but don't let it get too hot. Melt partially then whisk or stir with a fork to melt the rest.

Into a large mixing bowl whisk together the flour, sugar, baking powder and salt. With mixer on low speed add in melted butter and vegetable oil, beat until crumbly. Next beat in vanilla extract and the egg. Then turn up on high speed to mix completely until solid dough forms.

Transfer mixture to baking pan. Break up dough into pieces and distribute evenly in bottom of pan. With palm of hand press pieces down and together until it forms a solid and even bottom crust. Set aside.

Step 4: Make the filling
Stir powdered sugar with a fork to aerate a little before measuring. Then scoop out with measuring cup and level off. Place in medium bowl and set aside.

In a large bowl with electric mixer, beat softened Cream cheese, butter and salt until smooth. Beat in the 2 eggs one at a time and mix until creamy and smooth. Beat in the vanilla and almond extract.

Lastly add the powdered sugar in small increments, beating slowly at first so sugar doesn't fly everywhere. Once all the sugar is moistened beat on high until smooth. Scrape down sides of bowl to get all the sugar mixed in. Beat in the plumped cherries.
Pour this mixture evenly over the bottom layer. Spread with the back of a spoon or spatula to touch the edges and corners of the pan.

Sprinkle crumb topping evenly over batter. Very lightly with tins of a fork spread crumbs evenly over top and to the corners and edges.

Place the pan in the oven and bake at 350 for about 32 minutes. The edges should bet set and the center will be soft set, the topping should be a nicely browned and crisp. The center will firm up as it cools.

Cool on a wire rack for 1 hour. Cover and place in the fridge to finish firm up. Allow to chill at least 1 hour before slicing. Store tightly covered in the fridge.

For Blueberry Gooey Butter Cake: Replace cherries with blueberries. If you use fresh blueberries there's no need to plump them first. If you use dried blueberries plump them the same way as with the cherries.

Cranberry Cardamom Gooey Butter Cake

Soft coconutty crust topped with a cardamom spiced filling with plumped tart cranberries.

Ingredients

Bottom Layer:
2 cups all-purpose flour
1/2 cup granulated sugar
1/2 cup packed light brown sugar
1 tablespoon baking powder
1/2 teaspoon salt
1 teaspoon vanilla extract
2 large eggs, slightly beaten
1 stick real unsalted butter, melted but not hot
1/2 cup sweetened flaked coconut
1/4 cup vegetable oil

Filling:
3/4 cup dried sweetened cranberries, plumped and drained
1 (8 ounce) package Creamcheese, softened
1/4 cup coconut oil (or 4 tablespoons real butter, very soft and slightly melted)

2 large eggs
1 teaspoon ground cardamom
1/4 teaspoon ground nutmeg
1/4 teaspoon cinnamon
Dash of salt
1 teaspoon vanilla extract
3 cups powdered sugar

Directions

Preheat oven to 350F (177C). Grease the bottom and up the sides of a 9x13x2 baking pan.

Step 1: Make the bottom layer - A heavy duty or stand mixer is best for mixing the bottom layer as the mixture is thick.

Melt the stick of butter in the microwave but don't let it get too hot. Melt partially then whisk or stir with a fork to melt the rest.

Into a large mixing bowl whisk together the flour, granulated sugar, brown sugar, baking powder and salt. With mixer on low speed add in melted butter, vegetable oil, vanilla extract and the eggs. Then turn up on high speed and mix completely until a solid dough forms. Scrape down sides of bowl with spatula if needed. Next beat in the coconut until well incorporated.

Transfer mixture into baking pan. Break up dough into pieces and distribute evenly in bottom of pan. With palm of hand press pieces down and together until it forms a solid and even bottom crust.

Step 2: Plump the cranberries
In a small pot cover the dried cranberries with water and boil for 2 minutes until they plump. Drain well and set aside.

Step 3: Make the filling

Stir powdered sugar with a fork to aerate a little before measuring. Then scoop out with measuring cup and level off. Place in medium bowl and set aside.

In a large bowl with electric mixer, beat softened Cream cheese, coconut oil (or butter) until smooth. Beat in the 2 eggs one at a time and mix until creamy and smooth. Beat in the cardamom, nutmeg, cinnamon, salt and vanilla extract.

Lastly add the powdered sugar in small increments, beating slowly at first so sugar doesn't fly everywhere. Once all the sugar is moistened beat on high until smooth. Scrape down sides of bowl to get all the sugar mixed in. Beat in the plumped cranberries.

Pour this mixture evenly over the bottom layer. Spread with the back of a spoon or spatula to touch the edges and corners of the pan.

Bake at 350F for about 30-32 minutes until a golden color on top. Don't over bake, it should be soft set in the center and have a slight jiggle and the edges should be set. The center will firm up as it cools.

Allow to cool at least 1 hour at room temperature. Once it firms up, cut into small size pieces as they are very rich. Store tightly covered in the fridge or at room temperature. I think they taste best served at room temperature.

German Chocolate Gooey Butter Cake

A rich chocolate crust made with pecans and sweet German chocolate. Then filled with a creamy caramel and coconut filling.

Ingredients

Bottom Layer:
2 cups all-purpose flour
1 cup granulated sugar
1 tablespoon baking powder
1/2 teaspoon salt
1 stick real unsalted butter, melted but not hot
1 large egg, slightly beaten

1 (4-ounce) bar German's sweet baking chocolate, chopped into 1/2-inch pieces
1 teaspoon vanilla extract
1/2 cup chopped pecans

Filling:
1 (8 ounce) package Creamcheese, softened
1/2 stick (4 tablespoons) real unsalted butter, very soft and slightly melted
2/3 cup jarred caramel sauce (ice cream topping) or to make from scratch, recipe follows
2 large eggs
1/4 teaspoon coconut extract
1 teaspoon vanilla extract
1/2 cup flaked coconut
3 cups powdered sugar

Directions
Preheat oven to 350F (177C). Grease the bottom and up the sides of a 9x13x2 baking pan.

Step 1: If making your own caramel sauce, prepare it first so it can cool down to room temperature.

Homemade Caramel sauce:

1/4 cup real butter, don't sub margarine
Dash salt
1/2 cup packed brown sugar
1/3 cup heavy whipping cream
1 teaspoon vanilla extract

Directions
1. In a small saucepan melt butter and salt.
2. Add the brown sugar; whisk and cook until combined and thickened, about a minute or so.
3. Whisk in the whipping cream, until thoroughly blended another minute or so
4. Remove from heat

5. Mix in vanilla until combined.

6. Let come to room temperature before adding to recipe. If it starts to separate while cooling, whisk with a fork.

Store in fridge up to two weeks. Stir well before using.

This recipe makes about a cup, a little more than you'll need for this recipe. Freeze any leftovers up to a month.

Step 2: Make the bottom layer - A heavy duty or stand mixer is best for mixing the bottom layer as the mixture is thick.

Melt the chocolate by placing it in a very lightly greased microwave safe glass bowl. Heat it on medium high for about 1 minute to start with. Remove from the microwave and stir. Repeat heating at shorter intervals, 15 to 20 seconds, stirring in between, until the chocolate is completely melted and has a smooth consistency. Do not overheat or get any water in the chocolate. Remove the bowl from microwave and set aside until ready to use.

Melt the stick of butter in the microwave but don't let it get too hot. Melt partially then whisk or stir with a fork to melt the rest.

Into a large mixing bowl whisk together the flour, granulated sugar, baking powder and salt. With mixer on low speed add in melted butter and egg. Then turn up on high speed to mix completely until crumbly. Scrape down sides of bowl with spatula if needed. With mixer on low, beat in melted chocolate and vanilla extract, mixing well. Lastly beat in the pecans until mixed evenly throughout.

Transfer dough into prepared baking pan. Break up dough into pieces and with a rubber spatula press the dough down and together until a solid bottom crust forms.

Step 3: Make the filling

Stir powdered sugar with a fork to aerate a little before measuring. Then scoop out with measuring cup and level off. Place in medium bowl and set aside.

In a large bowl with electric mixer, beat softened Cream cheese, butter and caramel sauce until smooth. Beat in the 2 eggs one at a time and mix until mixture is creamy and smooth. Beat in the extracts then the flaked coconut.

Lastly add the powdered sugar in small increments, beating slowly at first so sugar doesn't fly everywhere. Once all the sugar is moistened beat on high until smooth. Scrape down sides of bowl to get all the sugar mixed in.

Pour this mixture evenly over the bottom layer. Spread with the back of a spoon or spatula so batter touches the edges and corners of pan.

Place the pan in the oven and bake at 350 for about 30 minutes until it turns a golden color on top. Don't over bake, it should be soft set in the center with a slight jiggle and the edges should be set. The center will firm up as it cools.

Allow to cool at least 1 hour at room temperature. Once it firms up, cut into small size pieces as they are very rich. Store tightly covered in the fridge or at room temperature. I think they taste best served at room temperature. Freezes well.

Gingerbread Gooey Bars with Lemon Cream

Soft spicy gingerbread crust with a creamy ginger filling topped off with tangy lemon cream.

Ingredients

Bottom Layer:
2 cups all-purpose flour
1 cup granulated sugar
1 tablespoon baking powder
1/2 teaspoon ground cinnamon
1/4 teaspoon ground cloves
1 teaspoon salt
1 teaspoon vanilla extract
1 large egg, slightly beaten

10 tablespoons real butter (1 stick plus 2 tablespoons) melted but not hot
2 tablespoons vegetable oil

Filling:
1 (8 ounce) package Creamcheese, softened
1/2 stick (4 tablespoons) real butter, very soft and slightly melted
2 large eggs
1/4 cup molasses
1 teaspoon vanilla extract
1 tablespoon tapioca flour
2 teaspoons ground ginger
Dash of salt
3 cups powdered sugar

Topping: Prepared Lemon Cream Sauce, recipe follows

Directions
Preheat oven to 350F (177C). Lightly grease the bottom and up the sides of a 9x13x2 baking pan.

Step 1: Make the bottom layer - A heavy duty or stand mixer is best for mixing the bottom layer as the mixture is thick.

Melt the butter in the microwave but don't let it get too hot. Melt partially then whisk or stir with a fork to melt the rest.

Into a large mixing bowl whisk together the flour, granulated sugar, baking powder, cinnamon, cloves and salt. With mixer on low speed add in melted butter, vegetable oil, vanilla extract and the egg. Then turn up on high speed and mix completely until a solid dough forms. Scrape down sides of bowl with spatula if needed.

Transfer mixture into baking pan. Break up dough into pieces and distribute evenly in bottom of pan. With palm of hand

press pieces down and together until it forms a solid and even bottom crust.

Step 2: Make the filling – A regular hand mixer will work for the filling
Stir powdered sugar with a fork to aerate a little before measuring. Then scoop out with measuring cup and level off. Place in medium bowl and set aside.

In a large bowl with electric mixer, beat softened Cream cheese and butter until smooth. Beat in the 2 eggs one at a time, mixing well after each addition. Beat until mixture is creamy and smooth. Beat in the molasses, vanilla extract, salt, tapioca flour, and ground ginger.

Lastly add the powdered sugar in small increments, beating slowly at first so sugar doesn't fly everywhere. Once all the sugar is moistened beat on high until smooth. Scrape down sides of bowl to get all the sugar mixed in.

Pour this mixture evenly over the bottom layer. Spread with the back of a spoon or spatula so batter touches the edges and corners of pan.

Place the pan in the oven and bake at 350 for about 30-35 minutes until golden on top. Don't over bake, it should be soft set in the center and have a slight jiggle. The center will firm up as it cools

Allow to cool at least 1 hour at room temperature. Once it firms up, cut into small size pieces as they are very rich. Store tightly covered in the fridge or at room temperature. I think they taste best served at room temperature. Just before serving drizzle with Lemon Cream Sauce. Freezes well.

Lemon Cream Sauce

1/4 cup granulated sugar
1 tablespoon cornstarch

1/3 cup evaporated milk
1/4 cup fresh squeezed lemon juice
1 tablespoon butter
2 drops yellow food coloring, optional

In a small saucepan mix together the sugar and cornstarch. Gradually stir in the milk. Cook over medium heat, stirring constantly, until mixture thickens and boils. Boil and stir 1 minute. Remove from heat. Whisk in lemon juice and butter. Stir in food coloring (if using) until it reaches desired shade of yellow. Let cool to room temperature then refrigerate. Once chilled, pipe on top of cooled gingerbread gooey cake using pastry bag or fill a ziptop style plastic bag and cut a corner off the bottom of the bag. Yields 1/2 cup lemon cream sauce.

Key Lime-Coconut Gooey Bars

Refreshing lime taste, this reminds me of a cheesecake and key lime pie combo with a gooey coconut crust baked in.

Ingredients

Bottom Layer:
2 cups all-purpose flour
1 cup granulated sugar
1 tablespoon baking powder
1 teaspoon salt
1 teaspoon coconut extract
1 large egg, slightly beaten
10 tablespoons (1 stick plus 2 tablespoons) real butter, melted but not hot
2 tablespoons vegetable oil
1/2 cup flaked coconut

Filling:
1 (8 ounce) package cream cheese, softened
4 tablespoons butter, softened
1 (14 oz.) can sweetened condensed milk
2 whole eggs

1 egg yolk
2 tablespoons tapioca flour
1/8 teaspoon salt
1/2 cup fresh squeezed key lime juice
1 tablespoon fresh squeezed lemon juice
1 teaspoon grated lime zest
1 teaspoon vanilla extract
3 cups powdered sugar
4 drops green food coloring, optional

Directions

Preheat oven to 325F. Lightly grease the bottom and up the sides of a 9x13x2 baking pan. Be sure your pan is at least 2 inches high, the filling puffs up when baking. Mine puffed up really high I was worried it would spill over. Even though it didn't, just to be on the safe side you might want to place a large cookie sheet underneath your baking pan on this one.

Step 1: Make the bottom layer-A heavy duty or stand mixer is best for mixing the bottom layer as the mixture is thick.

Melt the butter in the microwave but don't let it get too hot. Melt partially then whisk or stir with a fork to melt the rest.

Into a large mixing bowl whisk together the flour, granulated sugar, baking powder and salt. With mixer on low speed add in melted butter and vegetable oil, beat until crumbly. Next beat in coconut extract and the egg until egg is mixed in well. Beat in flaked coconut. Then turn up on high speed to mix completely until solid dough forms.

Transfer mixture into baking pan. Break up dough into pieces and distribute evenly in bottom of pan. With palm of hand press pieces down and together until it forms a solid and even bottom crust.

Step 2: Make the filling

Stir powdered sugar with a fork to aerate a little before measuring. Then spoon out into measuring cup, level off, place in medium bowl and set aside.

In a large bowl with electric mixer, beat softened cream cheese and butter until smooth. Beat in the eggs and egg yolk one at a time, mixing well after each addition. Mix until mixture is creamy and smooth. Beat in the sweetened condensed milk, tapioca flour and salt. With mixer on slow beat in the lime juice, lemon juice, lime zest and vanilla extract until well incorporated. Then turn up on high and beat for 2 minutes.

Lastly add the powdered sugar in small increments, beating slowly at first so sugar doesn't fly everywhere. Once all the sugar is moistened beat on high until smooth. You may need to scrape down sides of bowl to get all the sugar mixed in. If using food coloring, add the drops in now until it reaches a pale lime green color.

Pour this mixture evenly over the bottom layer. Spread with the back of a spoon or spatula so batter touches the edges and corners of pan.

Place the pan in the oven and bake at 325 for about 40-45 minutes until light golden on top and slightly darker gold around the edges. The filling will be set when done and shouldn't jiggle. The top will look just like a key lime pie or cheesecake.

Allow to cool at least 1-2 hours at room temperature. Then place in refrigerator until chilled at least 3 hours. Cut into small size squares as they are very rich. Store tightly covered in the fridge.

Lemon Gooey Butter Cake

Soft crust topped with a tangy lemon cream filling made with fresh squeezed lemon juice and zest.

Ingredients

Bottom Layer:
2 cups all-purpose flour
1 cup granulated sugar
1 tablespoon baking powder
1 teaspoon salt
1 teaspoon vanilla extract
1 large egg, slightly beaten
1/2 teaspoon lemon zest
10 tablespoons (1 stick plus 2 tablespoons) real butter, melted but not hot
2 tablespoons vegetable oil

Filling:
1 (8 ounce) package Creamcheese, softened
1/2 stick (4 tablespoons) real unsalted butter, very soft and slightly melted

2 large eggs
1-1/2 tablespoons tapioca flour
1/2 cup fresh squeezed lemon juice
1/2 teaspoon lemon zest
1/2 teaspoon vanilla extract
3 cups powdered sugar
4 drops yellow food coloring, optional

Directions
Preheat oven to 350F (177C). Lightly grease the bottom and up the sides of a 9x13x2 baking pan.

Step 1: Make the bottom layer -A heavy duty or stand mixer is best for mixing the bottom layer as the mixture is thick.

Melt the butter in the microwave but don't let it get too hot. Melt partially then whisk or stir with a fork to melt the rest.

Into a large mixing bowl whisk together the flour, granulated sugar, baking powder and salt. With mixer on low speed add in melted butter and vegetable oil and beat until crumbly. Next beat in vanilla extract, egg and lemon zest. Then turn up on high speed to mix completely until solid dough forms.

Transfer mixture into baking pan. Break up dough into pieces and distribute evenly in bottom of pan. With palm of hand press pieces down and together until it forms a solid and even bottom crust.

Step 2: Make the filling
Stir powdered sugar with a fork to aerate a little before measuring. Then scoop out with measuring cup and level off. Place in medium bowl and set aside.

In a large bowl with electric mixer, beat softened Cream cheese and butter until smooth. Beat in the 2 eggs one at a time, mixing well after each addition. Beat until mixture is creamy and smooth. Beat in the tapioca flour, lemon juice, lemon zest and the vanilla extract.

Lastly add the powdered sugar in small increments, beating slowly at first so sugar doesn't fly everywhere. Once all the sugar is moistened beat on high until smooth. Scrape down sides of bowl to get all the sugar mixed in. If using food coloring add it now until the batter reaches a pale yellow.

Pour this mixture evenly over the bottom layer. Spread with the back of a spoon or spatula so batter touches the edges and corners of pan.

Place the pan in the oven and bake at 350 for about 32-35 minutes until light golden on top. Don't over bake, it should be soft set in the center and have a slight jiggle but the edges should be set and lightly browned.

Allow to cool at least 1 hour at room temperature. Once it firms up, cut into small size pieces as they are very rich. Store tightly covered in the fridge or at room temperature. I think they taste best served at room temperature. Freezes well.

Lemon Sheet Cake with Strawberry Sauce

A moist tangy lemon sheet cake with a lemon mousse-like frosting then drizzled with a sweet homemade strawberry sauce. A delicious combination! This one is definitely 'company dessert' worthy.

Ingredients
1 stick unsalted butter
1/2 cup vegetable shortening
1/2 cup of water
2 cups sugar
2 cups all-purpose flour
1/2 teaspoon salt
1-1/2 teaspoon baking powder
1/2 cup of fresh squeezed lemon juice
1/2 cup of sour cream
2 eggs, slightly beaten
2 teaspoon of vanilla

Directions

Preheat oven to 350F (177C). Lightly grease the bottom and up the sides of a 9x13x2 baking pan.

Heat the butter, shortening and water in a large sauce pan just until the fats melt, don't boil. Whisk while it heats up. Once melted remove from heat. Now whisk in the sugar, flour, salt and baking powder. Once that's mixed in well, whisk in the lemon juice, sour cream, eggs and vanilla until batter is smooth and all ingredients are well combined.

Pour into prepared baking pan and bake for about 27- 28 minutes just until edges are golden and toothpick comes out clean. The top will feel springy when lightly touched.

Let the cake cool in the pan completely before frosting. While the cake cools, prepare the frosting.

Fluffy Lemon Frosting (Yields just enough to frost the top of a 9x13 sheet cake)

1/2 cup plus 2 tablespoons sugar
1/4 cup flour
1/8 teaspoon salt
3/4 cup evaporated milk
1 cup (2 sticks) butter cut into 1 tablespoon size pieces
2 teaspoons vanilla extract
1/4 teaspoon lemon zest

Cut up butter into pieces and leave out to soften slightly.

Mix sugar, flour and salt in saucepan. Gradually add evaporated milk. Cook on medium-low heat until mixture is very thick stirring constantly. Remove from heat and let cool at room temperature about 15 minutes. Beat in butter one piece at a time on high speed until mixture is smooth. Add vanilla extract and lemon zest and beat some more. Immediately frost cooled cake. Let frosted cake chill in the fridge about 30 minutes so the frosting can firm up a little before drizzling with strawberry sauce.

Note: If you prepare the frosting ahead of time, store in the refrigerator. When ready to use, let come to room temperature and beat again to fluff up before spreading on cooled cake. You can also place frosting in a plastic bag and cut off bottom corner and pipe small dollops over cake.

Drizzle strawberry sauce over the top of vanilla frosting in a thin stream. You can use a pastry bag or cut a small corner from a ziptop style plastic bag to pipe over frosting. Store in refrigerator tightly covered. Let set out about 15 minutes before serving so the frosting will soften slightly. Tastes best at room temperature.

Strawberry Sauce (Yields about 2/3 cup of sauce)

1 (10 oz.) carton frozen sliced sweetened strawberries, thawed
1 tablespoon sugar
3 tablespoons water
1 teaspoon lemon juice
1 tablespoon cornstarch
Pinch of salt
1/2 tablespoon butter
5+ drops of red food coloring

Instructions
To a medium sauce pan add all the strawberry sauce ingredients except butter and food coloring. Bring to a boil and boil gently while stirring with a wire whisk breaking down the strawberries as sauce thickens, about 10 minutes. Puree with an emulsion wand or blender until very smooth. Stir in butter until melted. Cooking the strawberries turns the sauce a rose color. If you prefer a deep red color, add food coloring until it reaches the desired color, about 5-6 drops. Place in fridge to cool slightly before drizzling over frosting.

Maple Spice Pecan Gooey Bars

Spice bars with pecans and real maple syrup baked in. A pleasing texture as you bite into a crispy topping then a creamy filling over a soft crust. Recipe also includes an alternative option for Date Maple Creams.

Ingredients

<u>Bottom Layer:</u>
2 cups all-purpose flour
1 cup granulated sugar
1 tablespoon baking powder
1 teaspoon salt
1 teaspoon vanilla extract
1 large egg, slightly beaten
10 tablespoons (1 stick plus 2 tablespoons) real butter, melted but not hot
2 tablespoons vegetable oil
1/2 cup pecans

<u>Filling:</u>
1 (8 ounce) package Creamcheese, softened

1/2 stick (4 tablespoons) real butter, very soft and slightly melted
1/2 cup real maple syrup *see option below
2 large eggs
1 teaspoon ground cinnamon
1/4 teaspoon ground ginger
1/4 teaspoon ground cloves
1/4 teaspoon ground nutmeg
1 tablespoon tapioca flour
1/2 teaspoon vanilla extract
1/8 teaspoon maple flavoring (for a more intense maple flavor)
3 cups powdered sugar
*Option: you can sub 1/2 teaspoon maple flavoring for the maple syrup and omit tapioca flour

Directions
Preheat oven to 350F (177C). Grease the bottom and up the sides of a 9x13x2 baking pan.

Step 1: Prepare the crumb topping

1/2 cup granulated sugar
1/4 cup flour
1/2 teaspoon ground cinnamon
1/8 teaspoon ground nutmeg
2 tablespoons butter

In a medium bowl whisk together the sugar, flour and spices. With a pastry cutter or food processor cut the butter into flour mixture until consistency is like fine bread crumbs or sand. Or you can just rub mixture between your fingers and thumb to mash the butter into the dry mixture. Once it's crumbly rub mixture between your hands until it resembles like sand. See image below. Set in refrigerator until ready to use.

Step 2: Make the bottom layer - A heavy duty or stand mixer is best for mixing the bottom layer as the mixture is thick.

Melt the butter in the microwave but don't let it get too hot. Melt partially then whisk or stir with a fork to melt the rest.

Into a large mixing bowl whisk together the flour, granulated sugar, baking powder and salt. With mixer on low speed add in melted butter and vegetable oil, beat until crumbly. Next beat in vanilla extract, egg and the pecans. Then turn up on high speed to mix completely until solid dough forms.

Transfer mixture to baking pan. Break up dough into pieces and distribute evenly in bottom of pan. With palm of hand press pieces down and together until it forms a solid and even bottom crust.

Step 3: Make the filling
Stir powdered sugar with a fork to aerate a little before measuring. Then scoop out with measuring cup and level off. Place in medium bowl and set aside.

In a large bowl with electric mixer, beat softened Cream cheese and butter until very smooth. Next beat in the maple syrup. Beat in the 2 eggs one at a time, mixing well after each addition. Mix until mixture is creamy and smooth. Beat in the cinnamon, ginger, cloves, nutmeg and tapioca flour until well incorporated. Next beat in the vanilla extract and 1/8 teaspoon of maple flavoring.

Lastly add the powdered sugar in small increments, beating slowly at first so sugar doesn't fly everywhere. Once all the sugar is moistened beat on high until smooth. Scrape down sides of bowl to get all the sugar mixed in.

Pour this mixture evenly over the bottom layer. Spread with the back of a spoon or spatula so batter touches the edges and corners of pan.

Sprinkle crumb topping evenly over batter. Very lightly with tins of a fork spread crumbs evenly over top and to the corners and edges.

Place the pan in the oven and bake at 350 for about 30-35 minutes. Don't over bake, it should be soft set in the center and have a slight jiggle. The top will be dark due to all the spices so it won't be golden but should be darker around the edges and the edges should not jiggle, only the center should jiggle just slightly. The center will firm up as it cools.

Allow to cool at least 1 hour at room temperature. Once it firms up, cut into small size pieces as they are very rich. Store tightly covered in the fridge or at room temperature. I think they taste best served at room temperature.

For Date Maple Creams: Add 2/3 cups chopped dates to the crust ingredients and omit the pecans then bake as usual.

Mocha Hazelnut Gooey Cake

Dark chocolate fudge crust with a creamy hazelnut and espresso flavored filling.

Ingredients

Bottom Layer:
1-2/3 cups all-purpose flour
1 cup granulated sugar
1/3 cup unsweetened cocoa powder
1 tablespoon baking powder
1/2 teaspoon salt
1 teaspoon vanilla extract
2 large eggs, slightly beaten
1 stick real unsalted butter, melted but not hot
1/4 cup vegetable oil

Filling:
1 (8 ounce) package Creamcheese, softened
1/2 stick (4 tablespoons) real butter, very soft and slightly melted
2 large eggs
* 1 teaspoon espresso powder
1 teaspoon vanilla extract
1 teaspoon Hazelnut extract
3 cups powdered sugar

Directions
Preheat oven to 350F (177C). Grease the bottom and up the sides of a 9x13x2 baking pan.

Step 1: Make the bottom layer -A heavy duty or stand mixer is best for mixing the bottom layer as the mixture is thick.

Melt the stick of butter in the microwave but don't let it get too hot. Melt partially then whisk or stir with a fork to melt the rest.

Into a large mixing bowl whisk together the flour, granulated sugar, cocoa, baking powder and salt. With mixer on low speed add in the stick of melted butter, vegetable oil, vanilla extract and the eggs. Then turn up on high speed to mix completely until well combined and crumbly. Scrape down sides of bowl with spatula if needed.

Transfer mixture into baking pan. Break up dough into pieces and distribute evenly in bottom of pan. With palm of hand press pieces down and together until it forms a solid and even bottom crust.

Step 2: Make the filling
* Be sure to use espresso powder <u>for baking</u> versus instant espresso coffee granules. Using coffee granules will make it taste bitter.

Stir powdered sugar with a fork to aerate a little before measuring. Then spoon out into measuring cup, level off, place in medium bowl and set aside.

In a large bowl with electric mixer, beat softened Cream cheese and the 4 tablespoons softened butter until smooth. Beat in the 2 eggs one at a time and mix until mixture is creamy and smooth. Beat in the Espresso powder, vanilla and hazelnut extract.

Lastly add the powdered sugar in small increments, beating slowly at first so sugar doesn't fly everywhere. Once all the sugar is moistened beat on high until smooth. Scrape down sides of bowl to get all the sugar mixed in.

Pour this mixture evenly over the bottom layer. Spread with the back of a spoon or spatula so batter touches the edges and corners of pan.

Place the pan in the oven and bake at 350 for 32-34 minutes until a rich golden color on top. Don't over bake, it should be soft set in the center with a slight jiggle and the edges should be set. The center will firm up as it cools.

Allow to cool at least 1 hour at room temperature. Once it firms up, cut into small size pieces as they are very rich. Store tightly covered in the fridge or at room temperature. I think they taste best served at room temperature. Freezes well.

Oatmeal Raisin Gooey Butter Cake

Soft oatmeal raisin gooey cake sprinkled with a crispy brown-sugar topping.

Ingredients

<u>Bottom Layer:</u>
2 cups all-purpose flour
1 cup granulated sugar
1 tablespoon baking powder
1/2 teaspoon ground cinnamon
1/8 teaspoon ground nutmeg
1 teaspoon salt
1 teaspoon vanilla extract
1 large egg, slightly beaten
10 tablespoons (1 stick plus 2 tablespoons) real butter, melted but not hot
2 tablespoons vegetable oil
1/2 cup raisins
1/2 cup uncooked oatmeal (any kind will work)
Filling:
1 (8 ounce) package Creamcheese, softened

1 stick butter, very soft and slightly melted
2 large eggs
2 tablespoons milk
1 teaspoon vanilla extract
1/2 teaspoon ground cinnamon
1/3 cup raisins
1/2 cup oatmeal
3 cups powdered sugar

Directions
Preheat oven to 350F (177C). Lightly grease the bottom and up the sides of a 9x13x2 baking pan.

Step 1: Make the crumb topping and store in refrigerator until ready to use:

1/2 cup lightly packed brown sugar
1/4 cup flour
1/4 teaspoon ground cinnamon
2 tablespoons butter

In a medium bowl whisk together the brown sugar, flour and cinnamon. With a pastry cutter or food processor cut the butter into flour mixture until consistency is like fine bread crumbs or sand. Or you can just rub mixture between your fingers and thumb to mash the butter into the dry mixture. Once it's crumbly rub mixture between your hands until it resembles like sand. Store in fridge until ready to use.

Step 2: Make the bottom layer - A heavy duty or stand mixer is best for mixing the bottom layer as the mixture is thick.

Melt the butter in the microwave but don't let it get too hot. Melt partially then whisk or stir with a fork to melt the rest.

Toss raisins and oatmeal together in a small bowl and set aside.

Into a large mixing bowl whisk together the flour, sugar, baking powder, cinnamon, nutmeg and salt. With mixer on low speed add in melted butter and vegetable oil and beat until crumbly. Next beat in the vanilla extract and the egg. Next beat in the raisins and oatmeal. Then turn up on high speed to mix completely until solid dough forms.

Transfer mixture to baking pan. Break up dough into pieces and distribute evenly in bottom of pan. With palm of hand press pieces down and together until it forms a solid and even bottom crust.

Step 3: Make the filling
Stir powdered sugar with a fork to aerate a little before measuring. Then scoop out with measuring cup and level off. Place in medium bowl and set aside.

In a large bowl with electric mixer, beat softened Cream cheese and butter until smooth. Beat in the 2 eggs one at a time, mixing well after each addition. Beat until mixture is creamy and smooth. Beat in the milk, vanilla extract and cinnamon. Then mix in the raisins and oatmeal until well incorporated into the batter.

Lastly add the powdered sugar in small increments, beating slowly at first so sugar doesn't fly everywhere. Once all the sugar is moistened beat on high until smooth. Scrape down sides of bowl to get all the sugar mixed in.

Pour this mixture evenly over the crust. Spread with the back of a spoon or spatula so batter touches the edges and corners of pan.

Sprinkle the crumb topping over the batter and using the tins of a fork gently spread out evenly to the edges.

Place the pan in the oven and bake at 350 for about 36-38 minutes until the edges are set and the center has a very slight jiggle. The center will firm up as it cools.

Allow to cool at least 1 hour at room temperature then cover tightly and store in the refrigerator at least 4 hours or more. When ready to serve cut into small squares. Store tightly covered in the fridge. I think they taste best served at room temperature.

Peaches & Cream Gooey Butter Cake

This is like a creamy peach cobbler. Delicious texture as you bite through the crispy cinnamony topping, creamy filling and soft crust. Recipe also includes an alternative option for Green Apple Gooey Butter Cake.

Ingredients

Bottom Layer:
2 cups all-purpose flour
1 cup granulated sugar
1 tablespoon baking powder
1 teaspoon salt
1 teaspoon vanilla extract
1 large egg, slightly beaten
10 tablespoons (1 stick plus 2 tablespoons) real butter, melted but not hot
2 tablespoons vegetable oil

Filling:
1 cup peeled and grated fresh ripe peaches (or drained and grated canned peaches)

89

1/2 teaspoon ground cinnamon
1/4 teaspoon ground nutmeg
1 tablespoon tapioca flour
Dash of salt
2 teaspoons granulated sugar
1 (8 ounce) package cream cheese, softened
4 tablespoons melted butter
2 large eggs
1 teaspoon vanilla extract
3 cups powdered sugar
Prepared crumb topping, recipe follows

Directions
Preheat oven to 350F. Grease the bottom and up the sides of a 9x13x2 baking pan.

Step 1: Make the bottom layer - A heavy duty or stand mixer is best for mixing the bottom layer as the mixture is thick.

Melt the butter in the microwave but don't let it get too hot. Melt partially then whisk or stir with a fork to melt the rest.

Into a large mixing bowl whisk together the flour, sugar, baking powder and salt. With mixer on low speed add in melted butter and vegetable oil and beat until crumbly. Next beat in vanilla extract and the egg. Then turn up on high speed to mix completely until solid dough forms.

Transfer mixture into baking pan. Break up dough into pieces and distribute evenly in bottom of pan. With palm of hand press pieces down and together until it forms a solid and even bottom crust.

Step 2: Prepare the crumb topping

1/2 cup granulated sugar
1/4 cup flour
1/2 teaspoon ground cinnamon

1/8 teaspoon ground nutmeg
2 tablespoons butter

In a medium bowl whisk together the sugar, flour and spices.
With a pastry cutter or food processor cut the butter into flour
mixture until consistency is like fine bread crumbs or sand. Or
you can just rub mixture between your fingers and thumb to
mash the butter into the dry mixture. Once it's crumbly rub
mixture between your hands until it resembles like sand. See
image below. Set in refrigerator until ready to use.

Step 3: Make the filling
Stir powdered sugar with a fork to aerate a little before
measuring. Then scoop out with measuring cup and level off.
Place in medium bowl and set aside.

Add the grated peaches to a medium bowl. After grating they
will look like pureed peaches. Sift the cinnamon, nutmeg,
tapioca flour, salt and granulated sugar over the peaches and
stir well. Set aside.

In a mixing bowl beat cream cheese and butter until smooth.
Beat in the 2 eggs one at a time, mixing well after each
addition. Mix until mixture is creamy and smooth. Add vanilla
extract; mix until combined. Slowly add the powdered sugar in
several increments until all is mixed in.

With a rubber spatula scrape the peach mixture plus any juices into the cream cheese batter. Be sure you get all of the juice and spices from the bowl. Beat the peach mixture into the batter. Pour mixture over bottom layer and spread evenly so that it touches the sides and edges of pan.

Sprinkle crumb topping evenly over batter. Very lightly with tins of a fork spread crumbs evenly over top and to the corners and edges.

Place the pan in the oven and bake at 350 for about 35-38 minutes. The center will be soft set, the edges should bet set and topping should be nicely browned and crisp. The center will firm up as it cools.

Cool on a wire rack for 1 hour. Cover and place in the fridge to finish firming up. Allow to chill at least 1 hour before slicing. Store tightly covered in the fridge.

Green Apple Gooey Butter Cake – to make an apple cream dessert replace the peaches with one cup of peeled and grated green apples.

Peanut Butter and Chocolate Gooey Cake

Peanut butter crust with a fudgy chocolate filling

Ingredients

Bottom Layer:
2 cups all-purpose flour
1 cup granulated sugar
1 tablespoon baking powder
1 teaspoon salt
1 teaspoon vanilla extract
1 large egg, slightly beaten
10 tablespoons (1 stick plus 2 tablespoons) real butter, melted but not hot
2 tablespoons vegetable oil
1/2 cup peanut butter

Filling:
1 (8 ounce) package creamcheese, softened
1/2 stick (4 tablespoons) real butter, very soft and slightly melted
2 large eggs

1 teaspoon vanilla extract
1/2 cup powdered baking cocoa
3 cups powdered sugar

Directions

Preheat oven to 350F (177C). Grease the bottom and up the sides of a 9x13x2 baking pan.

Step 1: Make the bottom layer - A heavy duty or stand mixer is best for mixing the bottom layer as the mixture is thick.

Melt the butter in the microwave but don't let it get too hot. Melt partially then whisk or stir with a fork to melt the rest.

Into a large mixing bowl whisk together the flour, sugar, baking powder and salt. With mixer on low speed add in melted butter and vegetable oil, beat until crumbly. Beat in peanut butter. Next beat in vanilla extract and the egg. Then turn up on high speed to mix completely until solid dough forms.

Transfer mixture into baking pan. Break up dough into pieces and distribute evenly in bottom of pan. With palm of hand press pieces down and together until it forms a solid and even bottom crust.

Step 2: Make the filling
Stir powdered sugar with a fork to aerate a little before measuring. Then spoon out into measuring cup, level off, place in medium bowl. Stir in the 1/2 cup cocoa. Sift together and set aside.

In a large bowl with electric mixer, beat softened cream cheese and the 4 tablespoons softened butter until smooth. Beat in the 2 eggs one at a time and mix until mixture is creamy and smooth. Beat in the vanilla extract.

Lastly add the powdered sugar/cocoa mixture in small increments, beating slowly at first so the mixture doesn't fly everywhere. Once all the sugar/cocoa is moistened beat on high until smooth. Scrape down sides of bowl often to get all the sugar/cocoa mixed in.

Pour this mixture evenly over the bottom layer. Spread with the back of a spoon or spatula so batter touches the edges and corners of pan.

Place the pan in the oven and bake at 350 for about 30-33 minutes until top looks dry, and edges are set and center will have a slight jiggle. The center will firm up as it cools. see pic below.

Let cool. Store tightly sealed. Best served at room temperature and cut into small squares.

Peanut Butter Gooey Bars

A sweet chocolate crust with a creamy peanut butter filling.

Ingredients

Bottom Layer:
1 (4-ounce) bar German's sweet baking chocolate, chopped into 1/2-inch pieces
2 cups all-purpose flour
1 cup granulated sugar
1 tablespoon baking powder
1 teaspoon salt
1 teaspoon vanilla extract
1 large egg, slightly beaten
1 stick real unsalted butter, melted but not hot

Filling:
1 (8 ounce) package Creamcheese, softened
1/2 stick (4 tablespoons) real butter, very soft and slightly melted
2/3 cups creamy peanut butter
2 large eggs
1 tablespoon tapioca flour
1 teaspoon vanilla extract
3 cups powdered sugar

Directions

Preheat oven to 350F (177C). Grease the bottom and up the sides of a 9x13x2 baking pan.

Step 1: Make the bottom layer -A heavy duty or stand mixer is best for mixing the bottom layer as the mixture is thick.

Melt the chocolate by placing it in a microwave safe glass bowl. Heat it on medium high for about 1 minute to start with. Remove from the microwave and stir. Repeat heating at shorter intervals, 15 to 20 seconds, stirring in between, until the chocolate is completely melted and has a smooth consistency. Do not overheat or get any water in the chocolate. Remove the bowl from microwave and set aside until ready to use.

Melt the stick of butter in the microwave but don't let it get too hot. Melt partially then whisk or stir with a fork to melt the rest.

Into a large mixing bowl whisk together the flour, granulated sugar, baking powder and salt. Beat in melted butter until mixture is crumbly then add the egg and beat until well mixed. Then turn up on high speed to mix completely. Scrape down sides of bowl with spatula if needed. Add in melted chocolate and vanilla and mix until it forms a solid dough.

Transfer dough into prepared baking pan. Break up dough into pieces and with hands press down firmly until a solid bottom crust forms. Flatten out with palms of hands until the dough feels smooth and even.

Step 2: Make the filling

Stir powdered sugar with a fork to aerate a little before measuring. Then scoop out with measuring cup and level off. Place in medium bowl and set aside.

In a large bowl with electric mixer, beat softened Cream cheese, butter and peanut butter on high speed until smooth. Scrape down sides of bowl if needed. Beat in the 2 eggs one at a time, mixing well after each addition. Mix until mixture is creamy and smooth. Beat in the tapioca flour and vanilla extract.

Lastly add the powdered sugar in small increments, beating slowly at first so sugar doesn't fly everywhere. Once all the sugar is moistened beat on high until smooth. Scrape down sides of bowl to get all the sugar mixed in.

Pour this mixture evenly over the bottom layer. Spread with the back of a spoon or spatula so batter touches the edges and corners of pan.

Place the pan in the oven and bake at 350 for about 27-29 minutes until a deep golden on top. Don't over bake, it should be soft set in the center and have a slight jiggle and the edges should be set. The center will firm up as it cools.

Allow to cool at least 1 hour at room temperature. Place in the fridge a while to firm up. Once it firms up, cut into small size pieces as they are very rich. Store tightly covered in the fridge or at room temperature. I think they taste best served at room temperature. Freezes well.

Pecan Pie Gooey Butter Cake

Soft bottom crust filled with a sweet creamy and nutty filling that bakes up soft and gooey. This tastes like a combo pecan pie/cake, it's a little of both and oh so good.

Ingredients

Bottom Layer:
2 cups all-purpose flour
1 cup granulated sugar
1 tablespoon baking powder
1 teaspoon salt
1 teaspoon vanilla extract
1 large egg, slightly beaten
10 tablespoons (1 stick plus 2 tablespoons) real butter, melted but not hot
2 tablespoons vegetable oil

Filling:
1 (8 ounce) package Creamcheese, softened
1/2 stick (4 tablespoons) real butter, very soft and slightly melted
1/2 cup dark Karo syrup

2 large eggs
1 tablespoon tapioca flour
1/8 teaspoon of salt
1 teaspoon vanilla extract
3 cups powdered sugar
1 cup chopped pecans

Directions
Preheat oven to 350F (177C). Grease the bottom and up the sides of a 9x13x2 baking pan.

Step 1: Make the bottom layer - A heavy duty or stand mixer is best for mixing the bottom layer as the mixture is thick.

Melt the butter in the microwave but don't let it get too hot. Melt partially then whisk or stir with a fork to melt the rest.

Into a large mixing bowl whisk together the flour, sugar, baking powder and salt. With mixer on low speed add in melted butter and vegetable oil, beat until crumbly. Next beat in vanilla extract and the egg. Then turn up on high speed to mix completely until solid dough forms.

Transfer mixture into baking pan. Break up dough into pieces and distribute evenly in bottom of pan. With palm of hand press pieces down and together until it forms a solid and even bottom crust.

Step 2: Make the filling
Stir powdered sugar with a fork to aerate a little before measuring. Then scoop out with measuring cup and level off. Place in medium bowl and set aside.

In a large bowl with electric mixer, beat softened Cream cheese and butter until smooth. Beat in Karo syrup until smooth. Beat in the 2 eggs one at a time, mixing well after each addition. Mix until mixture is creamy and smooth. Beat in the tapioca flour, salt and the vanilla extract.

Add the powdered sugar in small increments, beating slowly at first so sugar doesn't fly everywhere. Once all the sugar is moistened beat on high until smooth. Scrape down sides of bowl to get all the sugar mixed in. Beat in the cup of pecans until evenly distributed throughout dough.

Pour this mixture evenly over the bottom layer. Spread with the back of a spoon or spatula so batter touches the edges and corners of pan.

Place the pan in the oven and bake at 350 for about 30-35 minutes until golden on top. Don't over bake, it should be soft set in the center and have a slight jiggle and the edges should be set. The center will firm up as it cools.

Allow to cool at least 1 hour at room temperature. Place in the fridge to finish firming up. Store tightly covered in the fridge. I think these taste best the next day. These bars are very gooey and very delicious and I'd recommend eating with a fork instead of cutting into bars for finger food. Freezes well.

Peppermint Gooey Butter Cake

Soft bottom crust with a peppermint filling. Uses real ground peppermint sprinkled over the top that melts into the gooey filling for a delicious soft gooey minty treat.

Ingredients

<u>Bottom Layer:</u>
2 cups all-purpose flour
1 cup granulated sugar
1 tablespoon baking powder
1 teaspoon salt
1 teaspoon vanilla extract
3 large egg whites, slightly beaten
10 tablespoons real butter (1 stick plus 2 tablespoons), melted but not hot
2 tablespoons vegetable oil

<u>Filling:</u>
1 (8 ounce) package Creamcheese, softened
1/2 stick (4 tablespoons) real butter, very soft and slightly melted
2 large eggs

1 teaspoon vanilla extract
1/2 teaspoon peppermint extract, I used Watkins
3 cups powdered sugar
* 1/4 cup finely ground peppermint candies or chopped peppermint baking chips

Directions
Preheat oven to 350F (177C). Lightly grease the bottom and up the sides of a 9x13x2 baking pan.

* Grind about 1/2 cup of any inexpensive peppermints in a food processor until powdery, it will make about 1/4 cup ground peppermint. See image below. This will be sprinkled over the top after the cake is done. You can use peppermint baking chips instead but since they are a seasonal item so you may not be able to find them until the holidays roll around.

Step 1: Make the bottom layer - A heavy duty or stand mixer is best for mixing the bottom layer as the mixture is thick.

Melt the butter in the microwave but don't let it get too hot. Melt partially then whisk or stir with a fork to melt the rest.

Into a large mixing bowl whisk together the flour, granulated sugar, baking powder and salt. With mixer on low speed add in melted butter, vegetable oil, vanilla extract and the 3 egg whites. Then turn up on high speed to mix completely until solid dough forms.

Transfer mixture into baking pan. Break up dough into pieces and distribute evenly in bottom of pan. With palm of hand press pieces down and together until it forms a solid and even bottom crust. Use knuckles to press dough into corners.

Step 2: Make the filling
Stir powdered sugar with a fork to aerate a little before measuring. Then scoop out with measuring cup and level off. Place in medium bowl and set aside.

In a large bowl with electric mixer, beat softened Cream cheese and butter until smooth. Beat in the 2 eggs one at a time, mixing well after each addition. Mix until mixture is creamy and smooth. Beat in the extracts.

Lastly add the powdered sugar in small increments, beating slowly at first so sugar doesn't fly everywhere. Once all the sugar is moistened beat on high until smooth. Scrape down sides of bowl to get all the sugar mixed in.

Pour this mixture evenly over the bottom layer. Spread with the back of a spoon or spatula so batter touches the edges and corners of pan.

Place the pan in the oven and bake at 350 for about 28 minutes until golden on top. Don't over bake, it should be soft set in the center and have a slight jiggle and the edges should be set. The center will firm up as it cools.

Remove from oven and while still warm sprinkle the ground peppermint candy or peppermint baking chips over the top. You may not need all of it just a light sprinkle to cover the top. Return to oven for 30 seconds so it will melt slightly. Remove from oven and cover loosely with aluminum foil for 20 minutes. Remove the foil and with a knife or metal spatula make score marks through the candy layer where you will be cutting later.

Let cool to room temperature about an hour. Once it's cooled cover tightly and set in the refrigerator at least 2 hours or more. The ground peppermint candy layer will soften in the fridge so you'll be able to cut through it.

Cut into small size pieces as they are very rich. Freezes well.

Pink Champagne Gooey Bars

Soft cake crust with white chocolate chips filled with a creamy filling made with real pink champagne.

Ingredients

Bottom Crust Layer:
2 cups all-purpose flour
1 cup granulated sugar
1 tablespoon baking powder
1 teaspoon salt
10 tablespoons (1 stick plus 2 tablespoons) real butter, melted but not hot
1 large egg, slightly beaten
2 tablespoons vegetable oil
1 teaspoon vanilla extract
3/4 cups white chocolate chips

Filling:
1 (8 ounce) package cream cheese, softened

1/2 stick (4 tablespoons) real butter, very soft and slightly melted
2 large eggs
1 teaspoon vanilla extract
1/2 cup pink champagne
1 tablespoon tapioca flour
Dash of salt
3 cups powdered sugar
3-5 drops red food coloring

Directions
Preheat oven to 350F (177C). Lightly grease the bottom and up the sides of a 9x13x2 baking pan.

Step 1: Make the bottom layer - A heavy duty or stand mixer is best for mixing the batter and filling as the mixture is thick.

Melt butter in the microwave but don't let it get too hot. Melt partially then whisk or stir with a fork to melt the rest.

Into a large mixing bowl whisk together the flour, granulated sugar, baking powder and salt. With mixer on low speed add in melted butter, vegetable oil, vanilla extract and the egg. Then turn up on high speed to mix completely. Mix in in the white chocolate chips.

Transfer dough mixture into prepared baking pan. Pat down gently with hands of use a rubber spatula to flatten and even out until the bottom feels smooth and even.

Step 2: Make the filling
Measure out powdered sugar and place in a separate bowl. Before measuring, stir powdered sugar to aerate a little then scoop out into measuring cup and level off with a flat edge. Set aside.

In a large bowl with electric mixer, beat cream cheese and butter until smooth. Beat in the eggs one at a time until well mixed. Beat in the vanilla extract, pink champagne, tapioca flour and salt. Mix until well combined, about a minute.

Lastly add the powdered sugar in small increments, beating slowly at first then beat on high until smooth. You may need to scrape down sides of bowl to get all the sugar mixed in. Add red food coloring and beat until color is a pale pink and uniform throughout the batter. Beat on high about 30 seconds.

Pour this mixture evenly over the bottom layer. Spread with the back of a spoon or spatula so batter touches the edges and corners of pan. Shake pan side to side to help distribute batter evenly.

Bake at 350 for about 30-34 minutes until a rich golden color on top. Don't over bake, it should be soft set in the center with a slight jiggle and the edges should be set. The center will firm up as it cools.

Allow to cool at least 1 hour at room temperature. Once it firms up, cut into small size pieces as they are very rich. Can be stored at room temperature or kept in the fridge. I think the flavor is best when served at room temperature. Freezes well.

Pumpkin Pie Gooey Bars

A soft crust with chocolate chips baked in and topped with a warm spicy pumpkin filling.

Ingredients

Bottom Layer:
2 cups all-purpose flour
1 cup granulated sugar
1 tablespoon baking powder
1 teaspoon salt
1 teaspoon vanilla extract
1 large egg, slightly beaten
10 tablespoons (1 stick plus 2 tablespoons) real butter, melted but not hot
2 tablespoons vegetable oil
1/2 cup semi-sweet mini chocolate chips

Filling:
1 (8 ounce) package Creamcheese, softened
1/2 stick (4 tablespoons) real butter, very soft and slightly melted
2/3 cup solid pack canned pumpkin (or your own fresh cooked)

2 large eggs
2 teaspoons vanilla extract
1/2 teaspoon ginger *
1 teaspoon cinnamon *
1/8 teaspoon cloves *
1/8 teaspoon nutmeg *
1 tablespoon tapioca flour
3 cups powdered sugar
 *Instead of these 4 spices you can just use 1-3/4 teaspoons
pumpkin pie spice

Directions
Preheat oven to 350F (177C). Lightly grease the bottom and
up the sides of a 9x13x2 baking pan.

Step 1: Make the bottom layer - A heavy duty or stand
mixer is best for mixing the bottom layer as the mixture is
thick.

Melt the butter in the microwave but don't let it get too hot.
Melt partially then whisk or stir with a fork to melt the rest.

Into a large mixing bowl whisk together the flour, sugar, baking
powder and salt. With mixer on low speed add in melted butter
and vegetable oil, beat until crumbly. Next beat in vanilla
extract and the egg. Then turn up on high speed to mix
completely until solid dough forms. Beat in the chocolate
chips.

Transfer mixture to baking pan. Break up dough into pieces
and distribute evenly in bottom of pan. With palm of hand
press pieces down and together until it forms a solid and even
bottom crust.

Step 2: Make the filling
Stir powdered sugar with a fork to aerate a little before
measuring. Then scoop out with measuring cup and level off.
Place in medium bowl and set aside.

In a large bowl with electric mixer, beat softened Cream cheese, butter and pumpkin until smooth. Beat in the 2 eggs one at a time, mixing well after each addition. Mix until mixture is creamy and smooth. Beat in the vanilla extract, ginger, cinnamon, cloves, nutmeg and tapioca flour.

Lastly add the powdered sugar in small increments, beating slowly at first so sugar doesn't fly everywhere. Once all the sugar is moistened beat on high until smooth. Scrape down sides of bowl to get all the sugar mixed in.

Pour this mixture evenly over the crust. Spread with the back of a spoon or spatula so batter touches the edges and corners of pan.

Place the pan in the oven and bake at 350 for about 29-31 minutes until the edges are very light brown and the center has a few light brown spots on top and it looks like pumpkin pie. It will have a slight jiggle but dry to the touch and not sticky. The center will firm up as it cools.

Allow to cool at least 1 hour at room temperature then cover tightly and store in the refrigerator at least 4 hours or more. When ready to serve cut into small squares. Store tightly covered in the fridge. I think this taste best served at room temperature. This is one of my favorite recipes in this book, a fabulous dessert and perfect for the holidays.

S'mores Gooey Butter Cake

Graham cake crust full of chocolate chips filled with a sweet creamy vanilla filling.

Ingredients

Bottom Layer:
1 cup all-purpose flour
3/4 cup whole wheat flour
1/2 cup granulated sugar
1/2 cup packed light brown sugar
1 tablespoon baking powder
1/2 teaspoon cinnamon
1/2 teaspoon salt
1 stick real butter, melted but not hot
1/4 cup vegetable oil

1 tablespoon honey
1 teaspoon vanilla extract
1 whole egg
1 egg yolk - save the egg white for the filling
1/2 cup chopped pecans
1 cup milk chocolate chips

Filling:
1 (8 ounce) package Cream cheese, softened
1/2 stick (4 tablespoons) real butter, very soft and slightly melted
1 tablespoon light corn syrup
1/8 teaspoon salt
2 whole eggs + 1 egg white
1 tablespoon vanilla extract
3 cups powdered sugar

Directions
Preheat oven to 350F (177C). Grease the bottom and up the sides of a 9x13x2 baking pan.

Step 1: Make the bottom layer- A heavy duty or stand mixer is best for mixing the bottom layer as the mixture is thick.

Melt the stick of butter in the microwave but don't let it get too hot. Melt partially then whisk or stir with a fork to melt the rest. Set aside.

Add both flours, sugars, baking powder, cinnamon and salt to a large bowl. Whisk together or shake in a sealed container until well blended. Transfer to mixing bowl. Using the paddle attachment with mixer on low speed, mix in melted butter, vegetable oil, honey, vanilla extract, the whole egg and egg yolk into the dry ingredients and mix until combined. Turn up on high speed to mix completely until a solid dough forms. Scrape down sides of bowl with spatula if needed. Turn mixer to medium speed and mix in the pecans and chocolate chips until evenly distributed throughout the dough.

Transfer dough mixture to baking pan. Break up dough into pieces and distribute evenly in bottom of pan. With rubber spatula press pieces down and together until it forms a solid bottom crust.

Step 2: Make the filling

Stir powdered sugar with a fork to aerate a little before measuring. Then spoon out into measuring cup, level off, place in medium bowl and set aside.

In a large bowl with electric mixer, beat softened Cream cheese, butter, corn syrup and salt until smooth. Beat in the eggs and egg white one at a time until mixture is creamy and smooth, beat about 2 minutes until fluffy. Beat in the vanilla extract.

Lastly add the powdered sugar in small increments, beating slowly at first so sugar doesn't fly everywhere. Once all the sugar is moistened beat on high until smooth. You may need to scrape down sides of bowl to get all the sugar mixed in.

Pour this mixture evenly over the crust layer. Spread lightly with the back of a spoon or spatula to touch the edges and corners of the baking pan.

Place the pan in the oven and bake at 350 for 29-30 minutes until a light tan color on top, like a roasted marshmallow. Don't over bake, it should be soft set in the center with a slight jiggle and the edges should be set. The center will firm up as it cools.

Allow to cool an hour at room temperature. Once it firms up, cut into small size pieces as they are very rich. Serve warm for the full S'mores experience! Delicious with a tall glass of cold milk. Store tightly covered in the fridge or at room temperature. Best served warm or at room temperature.

Strawberry Gooey Butter Cake

Soft crust topped with creamy strawberry filling made with strawberry puree.

Ingredients

Bottom Layer:
2 cups all-purpose flour
1 cup granulated sugar
1 tablespoon baking powder
1 teaspoon salt
1 teaspoon vanilla extract
1 large egg, slightly beaten
10 tablespoons (1 stick plus 2 tablespoons) real butter, melted but not hot
2 tablespoons vegetable oil

Filling:
10 oz. carton frozen sliced sweetened strawberries, thawed
1 (8 ounce) package Creamcheese, softened

1/2 stick (4 tablespoons) real unsalted butter, very soft and slightly melted
2 large eggs
2 tablespoons tapioca flour
1/2 teaspoon salt
1 teaspoon vanilla extract
3 cups powdered sugar
5-6 drops red food coloring
2-3 fresh strawberry slices for garnish, optional

Directions

Preheat oven to 350F (177C). Lightly grease the bottom and up the sides of a 9x13x2 baking pan.

Step 1: Make the bottom layer - A heavy duty or stand mixer is best for mixing the bottom layer as the mixture is thick.

Melt the butter in the microwave but don't let it get too hot. Melt partially then whisk or stir with a fork to melt the rest.

Into a large mixing bowl whisk together the flour, sugar, baking powder and salt. With mixer on low speed add in melted butter and vegetable oil, beat until crumbly. Next beat in vanilla extract and the egg. Then turn up on high speed to mix completely until solid dough forms.

Transfer mixture to baking pan. Break up dough into pieces and distribute evenly in bottom of pan. With palm of hand press pieces down and together until it forms a solid and even bottom crust.

Step 2: Prepare Strawberries: Place the thawed strawberries in a blender or food processor and blend until strawberries break up and mixture is thick. Measure out 2/3 cups of strawberry puree and set aside.

Step 3: Make the filling

Stir powdered sugar with a fork to aerate a little before measuring. Then scoop out with measuring cup and level off. Place in medium bowl and set aside.

In a large bowl with electric mixer, beat softened Cream cheese and butter until smooth. Beat in the 2 eggs one at a time, mixing well after each addition. Mix until mixture is creamy and smooth. Beat in the 2/3 cups strawberry puree, tapioca flour, salt and vanilla extract until well combined.

Lastly add the powdered sugar in small increments, beating slowly at first so sugar doesn't fly everywhere. Once all the sugar is moistened beat on high until smooth. Scrape down sides of bowl to get all the sugar mixed in. If using food coloring add it now until batter reaches a pink color.

Pour this mixture evenly over the bottom layer. Spread with the back of a spoon or spatula so batter touches the edges and corners of pan.

Place the pan in the oven and bake at 350 for about 30-35 minutes until golden on top. Don't over bake. The edges should be set but soft set in the center and have a slight jiggle. The center will firm up some as it cools.

Allow to cool at least 1 hour at room temperature. Once it firms up store tightly covered in the fridge. Garnish the top with sliced strawberries if desired. The center will have a softer mousse like consistency so it's best eaten with a fork instead of cutting into finger food pieces.

Sweet Potato Pie Gooey Bars

Soft crust with warm spiced sweet potato cream filling with real marshmallows baked right in. Taste like a gooey sweet potato pie cake.

Ingredients

Bottom Layer:
2 cups all-purpose flour
1 cup granulated sugar
1 tablespoon baking powder
1 teaspoon salt
1 teaspoon vanilla extract
1 large egg, slightly beaten
10 tablespoons (1 stick plus 2 tablespoons) real butter, melted but not hot
2 tablespoons vegetable oil

Filling:
1 (8 ounce) package Creamcheese, softened
1/2 stick butter, very soft and slightly melted
2 large eggs
1 tablespoon vanilla extract
1 teaspoon ground cinnamon
1/4 teaspoon ground nutmeg
2 teaspoons tapioca flour
2/3 cups cooked and mashed sweet potatoes
1 cup miniature marshmallows
2 cups powdered sugar
Candied pecan halves for garnish

Directions
Preheat oven to 350F (177C). Lightly grease the bottom and up the sides of a 9x13x2 baking pan.

Step 1: Bake a large sweet potato until very tender. Peel and mash pulp until smooth. Measure out 2/3 cups and set aside until ready for use.

Step 2: Make the bottom layer - A heavy duty or stand mixer is best for mixing the bottom layer as the mixture is thick.

Melt the butter in the microwave but don't let it get too hot. Melt partially then whisk or stir with a fork to melt the rest.

Into a large mixing bowl whisk together the flour, sugar, baking powder and salt. With mixer on low speed add in melted butter and vegetable oil, beat until crumbly. Next beat in vanilla extract and the egg. Then turn up on high speed to mix completely until solid dough forms.

Transfer mixture into baking pan. Break up dough into pieces and distribute evenly in bottom of pan. With palm of hand press pieces down and together until it forms a solid and even bottom crust.

Step 3: Make the filling

Stir powdered sugar with a fork to aerate a little before measuring. Then scoop out with measuring cup and level off. Place in medium bowl and set aside.

In a large bowl with electric mixer, beat softened Cream cheese and butter until smooth. Beat in the 2 eggs one at a time, mixing well after each addition. Beat until mixture is creamy and smooth. Beat in the vanilla, cinnamon, nutmeg and tapioca flour until well combined. Next beat in the mashed sweet potatoes. Then beat in the marshmallows until evenly distributed.

Lastly add the powdered sugar in small increments, beating slowly at first so sugar doesn't fly everywhere. Once all the sugar is moistened beat on high until smooth. Scrape down sides of bowl to get all the sugar mixed in.

Pour this mixture evenly over the bottom layer. Spread with the back of a spoon or spatula so batter touches the edges and corners of pan.

Place the pan in the oven and bake at 350 for about 35-38 minutes until golden on top. Don't over bake, the edges should be set but it should have a slight jiggle in the center. The center will firm up as it cools

Allow to cool at least 1 hour at room temperature then store in the refrigerator. Garnish with candied pecan halves if desired.

Tres Leches Gooey Butter Cake

Enjoy the rich taste of the 'three milk cake' in these Tres Leches gooey bars. You will also find a cake mix version of this in Section 2 of this cookbook.

Ingredients

Bottom Layer:
2 cups all-purpose flour
1 cup granulated sugar
1 tablespoon baking powder
1 teaspoon salt
1 teaspoon vanilla extract
1 large egg, slightly beaten
10 tablespoons (1 stick plus 2 tablespoons) real butter, melted but not hot
2 tablespoons vegetable oil

Filling:

1 (8 ounce) package Creamcheese, softened
1/2 stick (4 tablespoons) real butter, very soft and slightly melted
2 large eggs
1/2 cup sweetened condensed milk
2 teaspoons vanilla extract (I used Mexican vanilla)
1 tablespoon dark rum or 1 tsp rum flavoring
1/2 cup evaporated milk
2 tablespoons tapioca flour
Dash of salt
3 cups powdered sugar
8 oz. tub whipped topping
Seasonal fresh berries for garnish

Directions

Preheat oven to 350F (177C). Grease the bottom and up the sides of a 9x13x2 baking pan.

Step 1: Make the bottom layer - A heavy duty or stand mixer is best for mixing the bottom layer as the mixture is thick.

Melt the butter in the microwave but don't let it get too hot. Melt partially then whisk or stir with a fork to melt the rest.

Into a large mixing bowl whisk together the flour, granulated sugar, baking powder and salt. With mixer on low speed add in melted butter and vegetable oil, beat until combined. Next beat in vanilla extract and the egg. Then turn up on high speed to mix completely until solid dough forms.

With a stiff rubber spatula transfer mixture to baking pan. Using the spatula press the dough down and spread across the bottom of the pan until even.

Step 2: Make the filling

Stir powdered sugar with a fork to aerate a little before measuring. Then spoon out into measuring cup, level off, place in medium bowl and set aside.

In a large bowl with electric mixer, beat softened Cream cheese and butter until smooth. On high speed beat in the 2 eggs one at a time and mix until mixture is creamy and smooth about 1 minute. Beat in sweetened condensed milk until smooth. Next beat in the vanilla extract, rum, evaporated milk, tapioca flour and dash of salt.

Lastly add the powdered sugar in small increments, beating slowly at first so sugar doesn't fly everywhere. Once all the sugar is moistened beat on high until smooth. Scrape down sides of bowl to get all the sugar mixed in.

Pour this mixture evenly over the bottom layer. Spread with the back of a spoon or spatula so batter touches the edges and corners of pan.

Place the pan in the oven and bake at 350 for about 35-37 minutes until golden on top. Don't over bake, it should be soft set in the center with a slight jiggle and the edges should be set.

Allow to cool at least 1 hour at room temperature. Once it firms up spread a layer (about half the tub) of the whipped topping over the top. Store tightly covered in the fridge or at room temperature. Cut into small squares and top with your berries before serving. Freezes well.

White Chocolate Strawberry Amaretto Bars

Soft bottom crust made with white chocolate chips then filled with a creamy sweet filling made with real Amaretto and a homemade strawberry swirl.

Ingredients

Bottom Layer:
2 cups all-purpose flour
1 cup granulated sugar
1 tablespoon baking powder
1 teaspoon salt
1 teaspoon vanilla extract
1 large egg, slightly beaten
10 tablespoons (1 stick plus 2 tablespoons) real unsalted butter, melted but not hot
2 tablespoons vegetable oil
2/3 cup white chocolate chips

Filling:
1 (8 ounce) package Creamcheese, softened
1/2 stick (4 tablespoons) real butter, very soft and slightly melted

2 large eggs
2 tablespoons tapioca flour
1 teaspoon vanilla extract
1/4 cup Amaretto liqueur
3 cups powdered sugar
Prepared strawberry sauce, recipe follows

Directions
Preheat oven to 350F (177C). Grease the bottom and up the sides of a 9x13x2 baking pan.

Step 1: Make the strawberry sauce and let cool:

Yields about 2/3 cup of sauce

Ingredients
1 (10 oz.) carton frozen sliced sweetened strawberries, thawed
1 tablespoon sugar
3 tablespoons water
1 teaspoon lemon juice
1 tablespoon cornstarch
Pinch of salt
1/2 tablespoon butter
5+ drops red food coloring, optional

Strawberry Sauce Instructions
To a medium sauce pan add all ingredients except butter and food coloring. Bring to a boil and boil gently while stirring with a wire whisk breaking down the strawberries as sauce thickens, about 10 minutes.

Puree with an emulsion wand or in a blender until smooth. Stir in butter until melted. Cooking the strawberries turns the sauce a rose color. If you prefer a bright red you can add food coloring until desired color is reached. Place sauce in fridge to cool a little before drizzling over cake.

Step 2: Make the bottom layer - A heavy duty or stand mixer is best for mixing the bottom layer as the mixture is thick.

Melt the butter in the microwave but don't let it get too hot. Melt partially then whisk or stir with a fork to melt the rest.

Into a large mixing bowl whisk together the flour, sugar, baking powder and salt. With mixer on low speed add in melted butter, vegetable oil, vanilla extract and the egg. Then turn up on high speed and mix completely until a solid dough forms. Scrape down sides of bowl with spatula if needed. Beat in the white chocolate chips until evenly distributed.

Transfer mixture into baking pan. Break up dough into pieces and distribute evenly in bottom of pan. With palm of hand press pieces down and together until it forms a solid and even bottom crust.

Step 3: Make the filling
Stir powdered sugar with a fork to aerate a little before measuring. Then scoop out with measuring cup and level off. Place in medium bowl and set aside.

In a large bowl with electric mixer, beat softened Cream cheese and butter until smooth. Beat in the 2 eggs one at a time, mixing well after each addition. Mix until mixture is creamy and smooth. Beat in the tapioca flour, vanilla extract and Amaretto.

Lastly add the powdered sugar in small increments, beating slowly at first so sugar doesn't fly everywhere. Once all the sugar is moistened beat on high until smooth. Scrape down sides of bowl to get all the sugar mixed in.

Pour this mixture evenly over the bottom layer. Spread with the back of a spoon or spatula so batter touches the edges and corners of pan. Drop nickel sized dollops of the strawberry sauce over the top of the batter and swirl a knife through each dollop to create a marbled design.

Bake at 350F for 28-30 minutes until a golden on top. Don't over bake, it should be soft set in the center and have just a slight jiggle done. The center will firm up as it cools.

Allow to cool at least 1 hour at room temperature. Once it firms up, cut into small size pieces as they are very rich. Store tightly covered in the fridge or at room temperature. I think they taste best served at room temperature. Freezes well.

Section 2 – Made with Boxed Cake Mixes

All the recipes in Section 2 begin with a boxed cake mix

Basic Gooey Butter Cake

A basic gooey butter cake. Soft buttery crust with a creamy vanilla filling with just a hint of nutmeg. Simple and delicious!You can find a homemade version of this in Section 1 of this cookbook.

Ingredients

Bottom Layer:
One box Yellow or Butter cake mix
1 large egg, slightly beaten
1 stick real butter, melted but not hot

Filling:
1 (8 ounce) package Creamcheese, softened
1/2 stick (4 tablespoons) real butter, very soft and slightly melted
2 large eggs
2 teaspoons vanilla extract
Dash of grated nutmeg (optional)

3 cups powdered sugar

Directions
Preheat oven to 350F (177C). Grease the bottom and up the sides of a 9x13x2 baking pan.

Step 1: Make the bottom layer - A heavy duty or stand mixer is best for mixing the bottom layer as the mixture is thick.

Melt the stick of butter in the microwave but don't let it get too hot. Melt partially then whisk or stir with a fork to melt the rest.

Empty cake mix into a large mixing bowl. With mixer on low speed mix melted butter and the egg into the cake mix. Then turn up on high speed to mix completely until consistency of thick sticky dough.

Using a stiff rubber spatula scrape mixture from mixing bowl and transfer into baking pan. Break up dough into pieces and distribute evenly in bottom of pan. With palm of hand press pieces down and together until it forms a solid bottom crust.

Step 2: Make the filling
Stir powdered sugar with a fork to aerate a little before measuring. Then spoon out into measuring cup, level off, place in medium bowl and set aside.

In a large bowl with electric mixer, beat softened Cream cheese and butter until smooth. Beat in the 2 eggs one at a time and mix until mixture is creamy and smooth. Beat in the vanilla extract and nutmeg if using.

Lastly add the powdered sugar in small increments, beating slowly at first so sugar doesn't fly everywhere. Once all the sugar is moistened beat on high until smooth. Scrape down sides of bowl to get all the sugar mixed in.

Pour this mixture evenly over the bottom layer. Spread with the back of a spoon or spatula so batter touches the edges and corners of pan.

Place the pan in the oven and bake at 350 for about 32 minutes until a golden color on top. Don't over bake, it should be soft set in the center with a slight jiggle and the edges should be set. The center will firm up as it cools.

Allow to cool at least 1 hour at room temperature. Once it firms up, cut into small size pieces as they are very rich. Store tightly covered in the fridge or at room temperature. I think they taste best served at room temperature. Sprinkle with powdered sugar just before serving. Freezes well.

Caribbean Cocktail Gooey Bars

Enjoy all the tropical flavors of a Caribbean cocktail in each luscious gooey bite!

Ingredients

Bottom Layer:
One Pineapple cake mix
1 large egg, slightly beaten
1 stick real unsalted butter, melted but not hot
1/3 cup flaked coconut

Filling:
1 (8 ounce) package Creamcheese, softened
1/4 cup coconut oil (or 4 tablespoons real butter, very soft and slightly melted)
2 large eggs
1-1/2 teaspoons coconut extract
1/2 cup fresh squeezed orange juice
1/2 teaspoon grated orange zest
1 tablespoon dark rum
1/8 teaspoon nutmeg
1-1/2 tablespoons tapioca flour

3 cups powdered sugar
Orange slices and maraschino cherries for garnish, optional

Directions

Preheat oven to 350F (177C). Grease the bottom and up the sides of a 9x13x2 baking pan.

Step 1: Make the bottom layer - A heavy duty or stand mixer is best for mixing the bottom layer as the mixture is thick.

Melt the stick of butter in the microwave but don't let it get too hot. Melt partially then whisk or stir with a fork to melt the rest.

Empty cake mix into a large bowl. With mixer on low speed mix melted butter and one egg into the dry cake mix. Beat in the flaked coconut and turn mixer up on high speed to mix completely until a solid dough forms. Scrape down sides of bowl with spatula if needed.

Using a stiff rubber spatula scrape mixture from mixing bowl and transfer into baking pan. Break up dough into pieces and distribute evenly in bottom of pan. With hands press pieces down and together until it forms a solid bottom crust. Flatten out with palms of hands until the bottom feels smooth and even.

Step 2: Make the filling
Stir powdered sugar with a fork to aerate a little before measuring. Then scoop out with measuring cup and level off. Place in medium bowl and set aside.

In a large bowl with electric mixer, beat softened Creamcheese and coconut oil (or butter) until smooth. Beat in the 2 eggs one at a time, mixing well after each addition. Mix until mixture is creamy and smooth. Beat in the coconut extract, orange juice, orange zest, rum, nutmeg and tapioca flour.

Lastly add the powdered sugar in small increments, beating slowly at first so sugar doesn't fly everywhere. Once all the sugar is moistened beat on high until smooth. Scrape down sides of bowl to get all the sugar mixed in.

Pour this mixture evenly over the bottom layer. Spread with the back of a spoon or spatula so batter touches the edges and corners of pan.

Place the pan in the oven and bake at 350 for about 30-35 minutes until golden on top and edges are light brown and set. Bake until just barely jiggles. It should be very soft in the center, it will firm up as it cools.

Allow to cool at least 1 hour at room temperature. Once it firms up, cut into small size pieces as they are very rich. Store tightly covered in the fridge or at room temperature. Garnish with orange slices, cherries or other fruit if desired just before serving. Freezes well.

Cherry Amaretto Gooey Bars

Cherry gooey bars with a hint of Amaretto liqueur! A delicious combo. Recipe includes a Chocolate Covered Cherry option at the end of recipe.

Ingredients

Bottom Layer:
One box Cherry Chip flavored cake mix
1 large egg, slightly beaten
1 stick real unsalted butter, melted but not hot

Filling:
1 (8 ounce) package Cream cheese, softened
1/2 stick (4 tablespoons) real unsalted butter, very soft and slightly melted
2 large eggs
1 teaspoon vanilla extract
1 tablespoon tapioca flour
1/4 cup Amaretto liqueur
3 cups powdered sugar
5 drops red food coloring, optional

Directions

Preheat oven to 350F (177C). Lightly grease the bottom and up the sides of a 9x13x2 baking pan.

Step 1: Make the bottom layer - A heavy duty or stand mixer is best for mixing the bottom layer as the mixture is thick.

Melt the stick of butter in the microwave but don't let it get too hot. Melt partially then whisk or stir with a fork to melt the rest.

Empty cake mix into a large mixing bowl. With mixer on low speed mix melted butter and one egg into the dry cake mix. Then turn up on high speed to mix completely until a solid dough forms. Scrape down sides of bowl with spatula if needed.

Using a stiff rubber spatula scrape mixture from mixing bowl and transfer into baking pan. Break up dough into pieces and distribute evenly in bottom of pan. With hands press pieces down and together until it forms a solid bottom crust. Flatten out with palms of hands until the bottom feels smooth and even.

Step 2: Make the filling
Stir powdered sugar with a fork to aerate a little before measuring. Then scoop out with measuring cup and level off. Place in medium bowl and set aside.

In a large bowl with electric mixer, beat softened Cream cheese and butter until smooth. Beat in the 2 eggs one at a time, mixing well after each addition. Mix until mixture is creamy and smooth. Beat in the tapioca flour, Amaretto and vanilla extract.

Lastly add the powdered sugar in small increments, beating slowly at first so sugar doesn't fly everywhere. Once all the sugar is moistened beat on high until smooth. Scrape down sides of bowl to get all the sugar mixed in. If using food coloring add it now and beat until batter turns a pretty pink color.

Pour this mixture evenly over the bottom layer. Spread with the back of a spoon or spatula so batter touches the edges and corners of pan.

Place the pan in the oven and bake at 350 for about 35 minutes until pinkish golden on top. Don't over bake, it should be soft set in the center and have a slight jiggle and the edges should be set. The center will firm up as it cools.

Allow to cool at least 1 hour at room temperature. Then chill in the fridge a while for easier slicing. Once it firms up, cut into small size pieces as they are very rich. Store tightly covered in the fridge or at room temperature.

I think they taste best served at room temperature. Freezes well.

For Chocolate Covered Cherry Amaretto bars: While cake bakes, pit a handful of fresh black cherries and cut into halves. You need enough halves to cover the top of the cake about 2 inches apart. When the cake comes out of the oven, press the cherry halves cut side down all over the top. Then make a chocolate ganache and pour a little on top of each cherry in a slow, thin drizzle. Let cool at room temperature then store in the fridge. Bring down to room temperature again before serving and sprinkle a tiny bit of powdered sugar over the top if desired.

To make the Ganache: Place 1/4 cup chopped bar chocolate that's labeled semi-sweet or preferably bittersweet (or use 1/4 cup dark chocolate chips) in a microwave safe bowl (like a Pyrex measuring cup) and add 1 tablespoon heavy cream, milk or canned milk. Microwave in 20 second intervals, stirring after every 15 seconds until melted. Because the cake is already very sweet try not to use sweet chocolate, if using bar chocolate go for the 60%-70% cacao range.

Chocolate Gooey Butter Cake

Dark chocolate fudge crust topped with a creamy cocoa filling. You can also find a homemade version of this in Section 1 of this cookbook.

Ingredients

Bottom Layer:
One box Dark Chocolate Fudge cake mix
1 large egg
1 stick real butter, melted but not hot

Filling:
1 (8 ounce) package Creamcheese, softened
1/2 stick (4 tablespoons) real butter, very soft and slightly melted
2 large eggs
1 teaspoon vanilla extract
1/3 cup powdered baking cocoa

3 cups powdered sugar

Directions
Preheat oven to 350F (177C). Grease the bottom and up the sides of a 9x13x2 baking pan.

Step 1: Make the bottom layer - A heavy duty or stand mixer is best for mixing the bottom layer as the mixture is thick.

Melt the stick of butter in the microwave but don't let it get too hot. Melt partially then whisk or stir with a fork to melt the rest.

Empty cake mix into a large mixing bowl. With mixer on low speed mix melted butter and the egg into the cake mix. Then turn up on high speed to mix completely until consistency of thick sticky dough.

Using a stiff rubber spatula scrape mixture from mixing bowl and transfer into baking pan. Break up dough into pieces and distribute evenly in bottom of pan. With palm of hand press pieces down and together until it forms a solid bottom crust.

Step 2: Make the filling
Stir powdered sugar with a fork to aerate a little before measuring. Then spoon out into measuring cup, level off, place in medium bowl. Whisk in the 1/3 cup cocoa and set aside.

In a large bowl with electric mixer, beat softened Cream cheese and the 1/2 stick of softened butter until smooth. Beat in the 2 eggs one at a time and mix until mixture is creamy and smooth. Beat in the vanilla extract.

Lastly add the powdered sugar/cocoa mixture in small increments, beating slowly at first so the powdered mixture doesn't fly everywhere. Once all the sugar/cocoa is moistened beat on high until smooth. Scrape down sides of bowl often to get all the sugar/cocoa mixed in.

Pour this mixture evenly over the bottom layer. Spread with the back of a spoon or spatula so batter touches the edges and corners of pan.

Place the pan in the oven and bake at 350 for about 30-33 minutes until a top looks dry. It will look just like a chocolate cake on top but a toothpick test doesn't work, it should be soft set in the center with a slight jiggle and the edges should be set. The center will firm up as it cools.

Allow to cool at least 1 hour at room temperature .Once it firms up, cut into small size pieces as they are very rich. Store tightly covered in the fridge or at room temperature. I think they taste best served at room temperature. Freezes well.

Creamy Mint Brownie Bars

Dark fudge crust with a delicious minty filling.

Ingredients

Bottom Layer:
One box Dark Chocolate Fudge cake mix
1 large egg, slightly beaten
1 stick real butter, melted but not hot.

Filling:
1 (8 ounce) package Cream cheese, softened
1/2 stick (4 tablespoons) real butter, very soft and slightly melted
1/2 teaspoon peppermint extract
1/4 teaspoon vanilla extract
2 large eggs
3 cups powdered sugar
6-8 drops green food coloring, optional

Directions
Preheat oven to 350F (177C). Grease the bottom and up the sides of a 9x13x2 baking pan.

Step 1: Make the bottom layer - A heavy duty or stand mixer is best for mixing the bottom layer as the mixture is thick.

Melt the stick of butter in the microwave but don't let it get too hot. Melt partially then whisk or stir with a fork to melt the rest.

Empty cake mix into a large mixing bowl. With mixer on low speed mix melted butter and the egg into the dry cake mix. Then turn up on high speed to mix completely until consistency of thick sticky dough. Scrape down sides of bowl with spatula if needed.

Using a stiff rubber spatula scrape mixture from mixing bowl and transfer into baking pan. Break up dough into pieces and distribute evenly in bottom of pan. With palm of hand press pieces down and together until it forms a solid bottom crust.

Step 2: Make the filling
Stir powdered sugar with a fork to aerate a little before measuring. Then spoon out into measuring cup and level off; set aside.

In a large bowl with electric mixer, beat softened Cream cheese and butter until smooth. Then add the two eggs one at a time and beat until mixed well about 1 minute. Beat in the peppermint and vanilla extract.

Lastly add the powdered sugar in small increments, beating slowly at first so sugar doesn't fly everywhere. Once all the sugar is wet, beat on high until smooth. You may need to scrape down sides of bowl to get all the sugar mixed in. If using food coloring, add it now and beat until a pale mint green color is even throughout the batter.

Pour this mixture evenly over the bottom layer. Spread with the back of a spoon or spatula so batter touches the edges and corners of pan.

Place the pan in the oven and bake at 350 for about 32-35 minutes until a golden color on top. Don't over bake, it should be soft set in the center with a slight jiggle and the edges should be set. The center will firm up as it cools.

Allow to cool at least 1 hour at room temperature. Once it firms up, cut into small size pieces as they are very rich. Store tightly covered at room temperature or in the fridge.

These bite size bars make a beautiful display on a platter or tiered candy stand. The pastel green color is very pretty against the dark chocolate color and would be nice for a St. Patrick's Day dessert. Freezes well.

Lemon Blueberry Gooey Bars

Lemon crust topped with a creamy fresh blueberry filling.

Ingredients

Bottom Layer:
One box Lemon cake mix
1 large egg, slightly beaten
1 stick real unsalted butter, melted but not hot

Filling:
1 (8 ounce) package Creamcheese, softened
1/2 stick (4 tablespoons) real unsalted butter, very soft and
slightly melted
2 large eggs
1 teaspoon vanilla extract
3 cups powdered sugar
1 pint (about 1-1/2 cups) fresh blueberries, rinsed and dry

Directions
Preheat oven to 350F (177C). Grease the bottom and up the
sides of a 9x13x2 baking pan. Be sure sides are well greased

or the blueberries will glue themselves to any ungreased areas.

Step 1: Make the bottom layer - A heavy duty or stand mixer is best for mixing the bottom layer as the mixture is thick.

Melt the stick of butter in the microwave but don't let it get too hot. Melt partially then whisk or stir with a fork to melt the rest.

Empty cake mix into a large mixing bowl. With mixer on low speed mix melted butter and the egg into the dry cake mix. Then turn up on high speed to mix completely until a solid dough forms. Scrape down sides of bowl with spatula if needed.

Using a stiff rubber spatula scrape mixture from mixing bowl and transfer into baking pan. Break up dough into pieces and distribute evenly in bottom of pan. With hands press pieces down and together until it forms a solid bottom crust. Flatten out with palms of hands until the bottom feels smooth and even

Step 2: Make the filling
Stir powdered sugar with a fork to aerate a little before measuring. Then scoop out with measuring cup and level off. Place in medium bowl and set aside.

In a large bowl with electric mixer, beat softened Cream cheese and butter until smooth. Beat in the 2 eggs one at a time and mix until mixture is creamy and smooth. Beat in the vanilla extract.

Add the powdered sugar in small increments, beating slowly at first so sugar doesn't fly everywhere. Once all the sugar is moistened beat on high until smooth. Scrape down sides of bowl to get all the sugar mixed in. Gently fold in the blueberries until evenly distributed throughout the batter.

Pour this mixture evenly over the bottom layer. Spread with the back of a spoon or spatula so batter touches the edges and corners of pan.

Place the pan in the oven and bake at 350 for about 30 minutes or until a rich golden on top. Don't over bake, it should be soft set in the center and have a slight jiggle and the edges should be set. The center will firm up as it cools.

Allow to cool at least 1 hour at room temperature. Once it firms up, cut into small size pieces as they are very rich. Store tightly covered in the fridge or at room temperature. I think they taste best served at room temperature. Freezes well.

Mocha Hazelnut Cream

Dark chocolate fudge crust with a creamy hazelnut and espresso flavored filling. You can also find a homemade version of this in Section 1 of this cookbook.

Ingredients

Bottom Layer:
One box Dark Chocolate Fudge cake mix
1 large egg
1 stick real butter, melted but not hot

Filling:
1 (8 ounce) package Creamcheese, softened
1/2 stick (4 tablespoons) real butter, very soft and slightly melted
2 large eggs
* 1 teaspoon espresso powder
1 teaspoon vanilla extract

148

1 teaspoon hazelnut extract
3 cups powdered sugar

Directions
Preheat oven to 350F (177C). Grease the bottom and up the sides of a 9x13x2 baking pan.

Step 1: Make the bottom layer - A heavy duty or stand mixer is best for mixing the bottom layer as the mixture is thick.

Melt the stick of butter in the microwave but don't let it get too hot. Melt partially then whisk or stir with a fork to melt the rest.

Empty cake mix into a large mixing bowl. With mixer on low speed mix melted butter and the egg into the cake mix. Then turn up on high speed to mix completely until consistency of thick sticky dough.

Using a stiff rubber spatula scrape mixture from mixing bowl and transfer into baking pan. Break up dough into pieces and distribute evenly in bottom of pan. With palm of hand press pieces down and together until it forms a solid bottom crust.

Step 2: Make the filling
* Be sure to use espresso powder for baking versus instant espresso coffee granules. Using coffee granules will make it taste bitter.

Stir powdered sugar with a fork to aerate a little before measuring. Then spoon out into measuring cup, level off, place in medium bowl and set aside.

In a large bowl with electric mixer, beat softened Cream cheese and the half stick of softened butter until smooth. Beat in the 2 eggs one at a time and mix until mixture is creamy and smooth. Beat in the espresso powder, vanilla and hazelnut extract.

Lastly add the powdered sugar in small increments, beating slowly at first so sugar doesn't fly everywhere. Once all the sugar is moistened beat on high until smooth. Scrape down sides of bowl to get all the sugar mixed in.

Pour this mixture evenly over the bottom layer. Spread with the back of a spoon or spatula so batter touches the edges and corners of pan.

Place the pan in the oven and bake at 350 for 32-34 minutes until a rich golden color on top. Don't over bake, it should be soft set in the center with a slight jiggle and the edges should be set. The center will firm up as it cools.

Allow to cool at least 1 hour at room temperature. Once it firms up, cut into small size pieces as they are very rich. Store tightly covered in the fridge or at room temperature. I think they taste best served at room temperature. Freezes well.

Nutty Date Gooey Bars

Delicious moist and gooey dessert with dates baked into the crust with a pecan and maple filling.

Ingredients

Bottom Layer:
One box French Vanilla cake mix
1 large egg, slightly beaten
1 stick real butter, melted but not hot
2/3 cups chopped dates

Filling:
1 (8 ounce) package Creamcheese, softened
1/2 stick (4 tablespoons) real butter, very soft and slightly melted
2 large eggs
1 teaspoon vanilla extract
1/8 teaspoon maple flavoring, I used Mapleine
Dash of salt
3 cups powdered sugar
2/3 cups chopped pecans

Directions
Preheat oven to 350F (177C). Grease the bottom and up the sides of a 9x13x2 baking pan.

Step 1: Make the bottom layer -A heavy duty or stand mixer is best for mixing the bottom layer as the mixture is thick.

Melt the stick of butter in the microwave but don't let it get too hot. Melt partially then whisk or stir with a fork to melt the rest.

Empty cake mix into a large mixing bowl. With mixer on low speed mix melted butter, egg and dates into the cake mix. Then turn up on high speed to mix completely until consistency of thick sticky dough.

Using a stiff rubber spatula scrape mixture from mixing bowl and transfer into baking pan. Break up dough into pieces and distribute evenly in bottom of pan. With palm of hand press pieces down and together until it forms a solid bottom crust.

Step 2: Make the filling
Stir powdered sugar with a fork to aerate a little before measuring. Then spoon out into measuring cup, level off, place in medium bowl

In a large bowl with electric mixer, beat softened Cream cheese and the half stick of softened butter until smooth. Beat in the 2 eggs one at a time and mix until mixture is creamy and smooth. Beat in the vanilla extract, maple flavoring and salt.

Add the powdered sugar in small increments, beating slowly at first so the powdered mixture doesn't fly everywhere. Once all the sugar is moistened beat on high until smooth. Scrape down sides of bowl often to get all the sugar mixed in. Beat in pecans until well incorporated.

Pour this mixture evenly over the bottom layer. Spread with the back of a spoon or spatula so batter touches the edges and corners of pan.

Place the pan in the oven and bake at 350 for about 34-36 minutes until center is a light gold color and has a slight jiggle and edges are lightly browned and set. The center will firm up as it cools.

Allow to cool at least 1 hour at room temperature .Once it firms up, cut into small size pieces as they are very rich. Store tightly covered in the fridge or at room temperature. I think they taste best served at room temperature. Freezes well.

Orange Date Anise Bars

Orange crust with dates filled with a creamy cheesy filling flavored with anise. Anise has a distinguished rich, deep flavor that pairs so well with orange. If you are looking for something out of the ordinary, this warm indulgence will be a delicious addition to your holiday or any day baking.

Ingredients

Bottom Layer:
One Duncan Hines Orange Supreme cake mix
1 large egg, slightly beaten
1 stick real unsalted butter, melted but not hot
1/2 tablespoon vegetable oil
2/3 cups chopped dates

Filling:
1 (8 ounce) package Creamcheese, softened
1/2 stick (4 tablespoons) real unsalted butter, very soft and slightly melted
2 large eggs
1/2 teaspoon vanilla extract
1/2 teaspoon pure anise extract *

Dash of salt
3 cups powdered sugar

* No more than 1/2 teaspoon, Anise can be very overpowering, just a little goes a long way.

Directions
Preheat oven to 350F (177C). Lightly grease the bottom and up the sides of a 9x13x2 baking pan.

Step 1: Make the bottom layer - A heavy duty or stand mixer is best for mixing the bottom layer as the mixture is thick.

Melt the stick of butter in the microwave but don't let it get too hot. Melt partially then whisk or stir with a fork to melt the rest.

Empty cake mix into a large mixing bowl. With mixer on low speed mix melted butter, vegetable oil and one egg into the dry cake mix. Then turn up on high speed to mix completely until a solid dough forms. Scrape down sides of bowl with spatula if needed. Beat in the dates until well incorporated.

Using a stiff rubber spatula scrape mixture from mixing bowl and transfer into baking pan. Break up dough into pieces and distribute evenly in bottom of pan. With hands press pieces down and together until it forms a solid bottom crust. Flatten out with palms of hands until the bottom feels smooth and even.

Step 2: Make the filling
Stir powdered sugar with a fork to aerate a little before measuring. Then scoop out with measuring cup and level off. Place in medium bowl and set aside.

In a large bowl with electric mixer, beat softened Cream cheese and butter until smooth. Beat in the 2 eggs one at a

time, mixing well after each addition. Mix until mixture is creamy and smooth. Beat in the salt, vanilla and anise extract.

Lastly add the powdered sugar in small increments, beating slowly at first so sugar doesn't fly everywhere. Once all the sugar is moistened beat on high until smooth. Scrape down sides of bowl to get all the sugar mixed in.

Pour this mixture evenly over the bottom layer. Spread with the back of a spoon or spatula so batter touches the edges and corners of pan.

Place the pan in the oven and bake for about 28-35 minutes until golden on top. Don't over bake, it should be soft set in the center and have a slight jiggle and the edges should be set. The center will firm up as it cools.

Allow to cool at least 1 hour at room temperature. Once it firms up, cut into small size pieces as they are very rich. Store tightly covered in the fridge or at room temperature. I think they taste best served at room temperature. Freezes well.

Orange Spice Gooey Butter Cake

A burst of orange and warm spices in every bite!

Ingredients

Bottom Layer:
One box Orange cake mix
1 teaspoon ground cinnamon
1/4 teaspoon ground ginger
1/4 teaspoon ground cloves
1/4 teaspoon ground nutmeg
1 large egg, slightly beaten
1 stick real unsalted butter, melted but not hot

Filling:
1 (8 ounce) package Creamcheese, softened
1/2 stick (4 tablespoons) real unsalted butter, very soft and slightly melted
2 large eggs
1 tablespoon tapioca flour
Dash flour
1/4 cup orange juice

1 teaspoon vanilla extract
3 cups powdered sugar

Directions
Preheat oven to 350F (177C). Lightly grease the bottom and up the sides of a 9x13x2 baking pan.

Step 1: Make the bottom layer - A heavy duty or stand mixer is best for mixing the bottom layer as the mixture is thick.

Melt the stick of butter in the microwave but don't let it get too hot. Melt partially then whisk or stir with a fork to melt the rest.

Empty cake mix into a large mixing bowl. Whisk in the cinnamon, ginger, cloves and nutmeg. With mixer on low speed mix melted butter and one egg into the dry mixture. Then turn up on high speed to mix completely until a solid dough forms. Scrape down sides of bowl with spatula if needed.

Using a stiff rubber spatula scrape mixture from mixing bowl and transfer into baking pan. Break up dough into pieces and distribute evenly in bottom of pan. With hands press pieces down and together until it forms a solid bottom crust. Flatten out with palms of hands until the bottom feels smooth and even.

Step 2: Make the filling
Stir powdered sugar with a fork to aerate a little before measuring. Then scoop out with measuring cup and level off. Place in medium bowl and set aside.

In a large bowl with electric mixer, beat softened Cream cheese and butter until smooth Beat in the 2 eggs one at a time, mixing well after each addition. Mix until mixture is creamy and smooth. Beat in the tapioca flour, orange juice, salt and vanilla extract.

Lastly add the powdered sugar in small increments, beating slowly at first so sugar doesn't fly everywhere. Once all the sugar is moistened beat on high until smooth. Scrape down sides of bowl to get all the sugar mixed in.

Pour this mixture evenly over the bottom layer. Spread with the back of a spoon or spatula so batter touches the edges and corners of pan.

Place the pan in the oven and bake at 350 for about 28-30 minutes until golden on top. Don't over bake, it should be soft set in the center and have a slight jiggle and the edges should be set. The center will firm up as it cools.

Allow to cool at least 1 hour at room temperature. Once it firms up, cut into small size pieces as they are very rich. Store tightly covered in the fridge or at room temperature. I think they taste best served at room temperature. Freezes well.

Pina Colada Gooey Bars

Pineapple flavored crust with coconut flavored filling!

Ingredients

Cake/Crust Layer:
 One box Pineapplecake mix
1 large egg, slightly beaten
1 stick real butter, melted but not hot.

Filling:
1 (8 ounce) package Cream cheese, softened
1/2 stick (4 tablespoons) real butter, melted but not hot
2 large eggs
1/2 teaspoon coconut extract
2/3 cup shredded coconut
3 cups powdered sugar

Directions
Preheat oven to 350F (177C). Grease the bottom and up the sides of a 9x13x2 baking pan.

Step 1: Make the bottom layer - A heavy duty or stand mixer is best for mixing the bottom layer as the mixture is thick.

Melt the stick of butter in the microwave but don't let it get too hot. Melt partially then whisk or stir with a fork to melt the rest.

Empty cake mix into a large mixing bowl. With mixer on low speed mix melted butter and the egg into the dry cake mix. Then turn up on high speed to mix completely until consistency of thick sticky dough. Scrape down sides of bowl with spatula if needed.

Using a stiff rubber spatula scrape mixture from mixing bowl and transfer into baking pan. Break up dough into pieces and distribute evenly in bottom of pan. With hands press pieces down and together until it forms a solid bottom crust.

Step 2: Make the filling
Stir powdered sugar to aerate a little before measuring then spoon out into measuring cup and level off with a flat edge; set aside.

In a large bowl with electric mixer, beat Cream cheese and butter until smooth. Add the two eggs one at a time and beat until mixed well. Beat in the coconut extract and shredded coconut. Lastly add the powdered sugar in small increments, beating slowly at first then beat on high until smooth. You may need to scrape down sides of bowl to get all the sugar mixed in.

Pour this mixture evenly over the bottom layer. Spread with the back of a spoon or spatula so batter touches the edges and corners of pan.

Bake for about 30-35 minutes until a rich golden color on top. Don't overbake, it should be soft set in the center with a slight jiggle and the edges should be set. The center will firm up as it cools.

Allow to cool at least 1 hour at room temperature. Once it firms up, cut into small size pieces as they are very rich. Store in fridge, serve at room temperature. Freezes well.

Red Velvet Gooey Butter Cake

A soft red velvet cake crust with a sweet cream cheese filling.

Ingredients

Cake/Crust Layer:
One box Red Velvetcake mix
1 large egg, slightly beaten
1 stick real butter, melted but not hot.

Filling:
1 (8 ounce) package Cream cheese, softened
1/2 stick (4 tablespoons) real butter, melted but not hot
2 large eggs
1 teaspoon vanilla extract
3 cups powdered sugar

Directions
Preheat oven to 350F (177C). Grease the bottom and up the sides of a 9x13x2 baking pan.

Step 1: Make the bottom crust -Use a stand mixer as the crust gets very thick.

Melt the stick of butter in the microwave but don't let it get too hot. Melt partially then whisk or stir with a fork to melt the rest.

Empty cake mix into a large mixing bowl. With mixer on low speed mix melted butter and the egg into the dry cake mix. Then turn up on high speed to mix completely until consistency of thick sticky dough. Scrape down sides of bowl with spatula if needed.

Using a stiff rubber spatula scrape mixture from mixing bowl and transfer into baking pan. Break up dough into pieces and distribute evenly in bottom of pan. With hands press pieces down and together until it forms a solid bottom crust.

Step 2: Make the filling

Stir powdered sugar to aerate a little before measuring then spoon out into measuring cup and level off with a flat edge; set aside.

In a large bowl with electric mixer, beat Cream cheese and butter until smooth. Add the two eggs one at a time and beat until mixed well about a minute. Beat in the vanilla extract.

Lastly add the powdered sugar in small increments, beating slowly at first then beat on high until smooth. You may need to scrape down sides of bowl to get all the sugar mixed in.

Pour this mixture evenly over the bottom layer. Spread with the back of a spoon or spatula so batter touches the edges and corners of pan.

Place the pan in the oven and bake at 350 for 30-35 minutes until a golden color on top. Don't overbake, it should be soft set in the center with a slight jiggle and the edges should be set. The center will firm up as it cools.

Allow to cool at least 1 hour at room temperature. Once it firms up, cut into small size pieces as they are very rich. Can be stored at room temperature or kept in the fridge. Freezes well.

Strawberry Banana Gooey Bars

A soft strawberry cake crust with a gooey banana cream filling. Just delicious and a hit with the kids too.

Ingredients

Bottom Layer:
One box Strawberry cake mix
1 large egg, slightly beaten
1 stick real unsalted butter, melted but not hot

Filling:
1 (8 ounce) package Creamcheese, softened
1/2 stick (4 tablespoons) real unsalted butter, very soft and slightly melted
2 large eggs
1 teaspoon vanilla extract
1 teaspoon banana extract (I used McCormick's)
3 cups powdered sugar
6 drops yellow food coloring, optional

Directions
Preheat oven to 350F (177C). Lightly grease the bottom and up the sides of a 9x13x2 baking pan.

Step 1: Make the bottom layer - A heavy duty or stand mixer is best for mixing the bottom layer as the mixture is thick.

Melt the stick of butter in the microwave but don't let it get too hot. Melt partially then whisk or stir with a fork to melt the rest.

Empty cake mix into a large mixing bowl. With mixer on low speed mix melted butter and one egg into the dry cake mix. Then turn up on high speed to mix completely until a solid dough forms. Scrape down sides of bowl with spatula if needed.

Using a stiff rubber spatula scrape mixture from mixing bowl and transfer into baking pan. Break up dough into pieces and distribute evenly in bottom of pan. With hands press pieces down and together until it forms a solid bottom crust. Flatten out with palms of hands until the bottom feels smooth and even.

Step 2: Make the filling
Stir powdered sugar with a fork to aerate a little before measuring. Then scoop out with measuring cup and level off. Place in medium bowl and set aside.

In a large bowl with electric mixer, beat softened Cream cheese and butter until smooth. Beat in the 2 eggs one at a time, mixing well after each addition. Mix until mixture is creamy and smooth. Beat in the extracts.

Lastly add the powdered sugar in small increments, beating slowly at first so sugar doesn't fly everywhere. Once all the sugar is moistened beat on high until smooth. Scrape down sides of bowl to get all the sugar mixed in. If using food coloring, add it now and beat until a pale yellow color is uniform throughout the batter.

Pour this mixture evenly over the bottom layer. Spread with the back of a spoon or spatula so batter touches the edges and corners of pan.

Place the pan in the oven and bake at 350 for about 34-35 minutes until golden on top. Don't over bake, it should be soft set in the center and have a slight jiggle and the edges should be set. The center will firm up as it cools.

Allow to cool at least 1 hour at room temperature. Once it firms up, cut into small size pieces as they are very rich. Store tightly covered in the fridge or at room temperature. I think they taste best served at room temperature. Freezes well.

Strawberry Gooey Butter Cake

Strawberry crust filled with a sweet cheesy filling.

Ingredients

Cake:
 One box Strawberry flavoredcake mix
1 large egg, slightly beaten
1 stick real butter, melted but not hot

Filling:
1 (8 ounce) package Cream cheese, softened
1/2 stick (4 tablespoons) real butter, melted but not hot
2 large eggs
1 teaspoon vanillaextract
3 cups powdered sugar

Directions
Preheat oven to 350F (177C). Grease the bottom and up the sides of a 9x13x2 baking pan.

Step 1: Make the bottom layer - A heavy duty or stand mixer is best for mixing the bottom layer as the mixture is thick.

Melt the stick of butter in the microwave but don't let it get too hot, just barely melted. Melt partially and stir with a fork to melt the rest.

Empty cake mix into a large mixing bowl. With mixer on low speed mix melted butter and the egg into the cake mix. Then turn up on high speed to mix completely until consistency of thick sticky dough.

Using a stiff rubber spatula scrape mixture from mixing bowl and transfer into baking pan. Break up dough into pieces and distribute evenly in bottom of pan. With palm of hand press pieces down and together until it forms a solid bottom crust.

Step 2: Make the filling
Measure out powdered sugar and place in a separate bowl. Before measuring, stir powdered sugar to aerate a little then scoop out into measuring cup and level off with a flat edge. Set aside.

In a large bowl with electric mixer, beat Cream cheese and butter until smooth. Add the eggs one at a time beating until mixed well. Lastly beat in the powdered sugar in small increments and beat about a minute or until smooth.

Pour this mixture evenly over the bottom layer. Spread with the back of a spoon or spatula so batter touches the edges and corners of pan.

Place the pan in the oven and bake at 350 for 32-35 minutes until a golden color on top. Don't overbake, it should be soft set in the center with a slight jiggle and the edges should be set.

Allow to cool about 1 hour at room temperature. Once it firms up, cut into small bite size pieces. Garnish with strawberry slices if desired. Can be stored at room temperature or kept in the fridge. They taste best served at room temperature. Freezes well.

Tres Leches Gooey Bars

Enjoy the rich taste of the 'three milk cake' in these Tres Leches gooey bars.
If you are not able to find Tres Leches cake mix in your area you can try our homemade version in Section 1 of this cookbook.

Ingredients

Bottom Layer:
One box Tres Leches cake mix (Duncan Hines)
1 large egg, slightly beaten
1 stick real unsalted butter, melted but not hot
1 tablespoon of water

Filling:
1 (8 ounce) package Creamcheese, softened
1/2 stick (4 tablespoons) real unsalted butter, very soft and slightly melted
2 large eggs

Dash salt
2 teaspoons vanilla extract
1 tablespoon dark rum
3 cups powdered sugar

Directions

Preheat oven to 350F (177C). Lightly grease the bottom and up the sides of a 9x13x2 baking pan.

Step 1: Make the bottom layer - A heavy duty or stand mixer is best for mixing the bottom layer as the mixture is thick.

Melt the stick of butter in the microwave but don't let it get too hot. Melt partially then whisk or stir with a fork to melt the rest.

Empty both packets from the cake mix (a packet of cake mix and a small tres leches milk packet) into a large mixing bowl. With mixer on low speed mix melted butter, water and the egg into the dry mix. Then turn up on high speed to mix completely until a solid dough forms. Scrape down sides of bowl with spatula if needed.

Using a stiff rubber spatula scrape mixture from mixing bowl and transfer into baking pan. Break up dough into pieces and distribute evenly in bottom of pan. With spatula press dough down into pan evenly until it forms a solid bottom crust. Flatten out with palms of hands until the bottom feels smooth and even.

Step 2: Make the filling
Stir powdered sugar with a fork to aerate a little before measuring. Then scoop out with measuring cup and level off. Place in medium bowl and set aside.

In a large bowl with electric mixer, beat softened Cream cheese and butter until smooth. Beat in the 2 eggs one at a

time, mixing well after each addition. Mix until mixture is creamy and smooth. Beat in the salt, vanilla extract and dark rum.

Lastly add the powdered sugar in small increments, beating slowly at first so sugar doesn't fly everywhere. Once all the sugar is moistened beat on high until smooth. Scrape down sides of bowl to get all the sugar mixed in.

Pour this mixture evenly over the bottom layer. Spread with the back of a spoon or spatula so batter touches the edges and corners of pan.

Place the pan in the oven and bake at 350 for about 35 minutes until golden on top. Don't over bake, it should be soft set in the center and have a slight jiggle and the edges should be set. The center will firm up as it cools.

Allow to cool at least 1 hour at room temperature. Once it firms up, cut into small size pieces as they are very rich. Store tightly covered in the fridge or at room temperature. I think they taste best served at room temperature. Freezes well.

Tropical Gooey Bars

Coconut flavored crust with a pineapple, coconut and rum filling.

Ingredients

Bottom Layer:
One box Coconut cake mix
1 large egg, slightly beaten
1 stick real unsalted butter, melted but not hot

Filling:
1 (8 ounce) package Creamcheese, softened
1/2 stick (4 tablespoons) real unsalted butter, very soft and slightly melted
2 large eggs
8 oz. can crushed pineapple, drained
2 teaspoons tapioca flour
Dash salt
1 teaspoon rum extract
1/2 teaspoon coconut extract
1/2 teaspoon vanilla extract
3 cups powdered sugar

Directions
Preheat oven to 350F (177C). Grease the bottom and up the sides of a 9x13x2 baking pan.

Step 1: Make the bottom layer - A heavy duty or stand mixer is best for mixing the bottom layer as the mixture is thick.

Melt the stick of butter in the microwave but don't let it get too hot. Melt partially then whisk or stir with a fork to melt the rest.

Empty cake mix into large mixing bowl. With mixer on low speed mix melted butter and the egg into the dry cake mix. Then turn up on high speed to mix completely until a solid dough forms. Scrape down sides of bowl with spatula if needed.

Using a stiff rubber spatula scrape mixture from mixing bowl into baking pan. Break up dough into pieces and distribute evenly in bottom of pan. With hands press pieces down and together until it forms a solid bottom crust. Flatten out with palms of hands until the bottom feels smooth and even.

Step 2: Make the filling
Stir powdered sugar with a fork to aerate a little before measuring. Then scoop out with measuring cup and level off. Place in medium bowl and set aside.

In a large bowl with electric mixer, beat softened Cream cheese and butter until smooth. Beat in the 2 eggs one at a time. Beat in pineapple, tapioca flour and dash of salt until mixture is creamy and smooth. Next beat in the extracts.

Lastly add the powdered sugar in small increments, beating slowly at first so sugar doesn't fly everywhere. Once all the sugar is moistened beat on high until smooth. Scrape down sides of bowl to get all the sugar mixed in.

Pour this mixture evenly over the bottom layer. Spread with the back of a spoon or spatula so batter touches the edges and corners of pan.

Place the pan in the oven and bake at 350 for about 30-35 minutes until a golden color on top. Don't over bake, it should be soft set in the center with a slight jiggle and the edges should be set. The center will firm up as it cools.

Allow to cool at least 1 hour at room temperature. Once it firms up, cut into small size pieces as they are very rich. Store tightly covered in the fridge. Serve at room temperature. Freezes well.

Tutti-Frutti Gooey Bars

A sweet, fruit flavored dessert with a mish mash of five fruit flavors including Grenadine syrup for a unique taste. A favorite with the kids too!

Ingredients

Bottom Layer:
One box Pineapple cake mix
1 large egg, slightly beaten
1 teaspoon banana extract
1 stick real unsalted butter, melted but not hot

Filling:
1 (8 ounce) package Creamcheese, softened
1/2 stick (4 tablespoons) real unsalted butter, very soft and slightly melted
2 large eggs
1 tablespoon tapioca flour

1/4 cup frozen orange juice concentrate, thawed (not mixed with water)
1 teaspoon vanilla extract
1/2 teaspoon coconut extract
3 cups powdered sugar
2 teaspoons Grenadine syrup

Directions
Preheat oven to 350F (177C). Lightly grease the bottom and up the sides of a 9x13x2 baking pan.

Step 1: Make the bottom layer - A heavy duty or stand mixer is best for mixing the bottom layer as the mixture is thick.

Melt the stick of butter in the microwave but don't let it get too hot. Melt partially then whisk or stir with a fork to melt the rest.

Empty cake mix into a large mixing bowl. With mixer on low speed mix melted butter, the egg and the banana extract into the dry cake mix. Then turn up on high speed to mix completely until a solid dough forms. Scrape down sides of bowl with spatula if needed.

Using a stiff rubber spatula scrape mixture from mixing bowl and transfer into baking pan. Break up dough into pieces and distribute evenly in bottom of pan. With hands press pieces down and together until it forms a solid bottom crust. Flatten out with palms of hands until the bottom feels smooth and even.

Step 2: Make the filling
Stir powdered sugar with a fork to aerate a little before measuring. Then scoop out with measuring cup and level off. Place in medium bowl and set aside.

In a large bowl with electric mixer, beat softened Cream cheese and butter until smooth. Beat in the 2 eggs one at a

time, mixing well after each addition. Beat until mixture is creamy and smooth. Beat in the tapioca flour, orange juice concentrate, extracts and the Grenadine.

Lastly add the powdered sugar in small increments, beating slowly at first so sugar doesn't fly everywhere. Once all the sugar is moistened beat on high until smooth. Scrape down sides of bowl to get all the sugar mixed in.

Pour this mixture evenly over the bottom layer. Spread with the back of a spoon or spatula so batter touches the edges and corners of pan.

Place the pan in the oven and bake at 350 for about 30-35 minutes until golden on top. Don't over bake, it should be soft set in the center and have a slight jiggle. The edges should be set.

Allow to cool at least 1 hour at room temperature. Once it firms up, cut into small size pieces as they are very rich. Store tightly covered in the fridge or at room temperature. I think they taste best served at room temperature. Freezes well.

If you enjoyed this e-book please consider giving it a review on Amazon.com!

Made in the USA
Columbia, SC
24 February 2022

56739138R00102